D0324332

NORTH CAROLINA'S
HISTORIC RESTAURANTS
and their recipes

NORTH CAROLINA'S HISTORIC RESTAURANTS

and their recipes

by Dawn O'Brien

Drawings by Debra L. Hampton

John F. Blair, Publisher
Winston-Salem, North Carolina

Revised Edition
Third Printing 1990

Drawings by Debra L. Hampton
Cover photographs by Bernard Carpenter
Composition by The Composing Room of Michigan
Manufactured by R. R. Donnelley & Sons

Library of Congress Cataloging in Publication Data

O'Brien, Dawn.
North Carolina's historic restaurants and their recipes.

Includes index.
1. Cookery, American—North Carolina.   2. Restaurants,
lunch
rooms, etc.—North Carolina.   3. Historic buildings—
North Carolina.   I. Title.
TX715.O'285   1983   641.5'09756   83–2831
ISBN 0–89587–067–3

ACKNOWLEDGMENTS **W**ords seem insufficient to describe my thanks to the chefs who whispered, "This is the secret," as they showed me how they prepare a prized recipe, and to the owners who shared their restaurants' histories with me.

Multiple thanks to my editor, Audrey Kirby, who kept my participles from dangling.

I also thank the artist, Debra Hampton, for her pen and ink renderings of the restaurants.

A very special thank-you goes to Marty Rawson, Artie Rockwell, and Bev Wachtel for helping me test, retest, and correct many recipes.

A salute to the guinea pigs who downed as many as eight recipes in one sitting: Linda High; Tommy Peters; Frank and Lee Kecseti; Betty Jo Gilley; Jessica and Dick Roubaud; my husband, John; and my daughters, Daintry and Heather. And also to my cookie aficionado, Martin Sokoloff.

The award for courage, care, and criticism goes to the members of my writers' support group: John Brooks, Tom Collins, Diane and Justus Harris, Mark Moss, Irvin Prescott, Jim Roberts, and Nancy Young.

You can't say too much about encouragement, and I got a lot of it from my mother and my sisters and friends who are too many to name but who know who they are.

This book is dedicated to my daughters, Daintry and Heather. When Daintry discovered the nature of this project, she spontaneously uttered, "You know, Mother, the worst that could happen is you might learn how to cook!" And then there was my dear Heather, so often a victim of my culinary efforts, who swallowed and asked, "Does this mean more of your fancy dodah meals?"

You see, prior to embarking upon this project, the only literary efforts my family connected me with were serious articles on health, the corporate climate, and public relations. My work was assigned, not chosen. It's a wonderful way to make a living, and for the most part I've enjoyed it. But when I began to notice my family's sly smiles when I attempted an ambitious recipe, I decided the time had come for me to exercise new options.

First, I approached my husband, and as the analytical person he is, he immediately wanted to know what I considered to be my credentials. I reminded him that I have a master's degree in communication from Wake Forest University, and that I have written dozens of training manuals and audiovisual programs for industry. He pointed out, however, that my education had not extended to the Cordon Bleu culinary institute.

Unsatisfied with his response, I decided to make a list. It read:
I like to eat.
I like to eat well.
I like to eat well in beautiful old restaurants.
I'd like to produce meals similar to those of gourmet chefs.
I'd like to stay thin—well, reasonably.

This time, bypassing my usually supportive family, I went to my friend Jan with my problematic idea. Let me tell you about good friends. They know how to lie lovingly and will then tactfully help you solve the problem. For instance, when I admitted that I was no real cook, Jan effusively exclaimed, "That's just not true. I've had excellent meals in your home."

"Yeah, but if it was good, it was probably one of my lucky accidents," I replied.

This is how she tactfully attacked my problem: "Look, you'll be going into the kitchen of every restaurant, where you can learn the tricks and secrets from the most experienced professional gourmet chefs in the state, right?"

"Right."

"You'll go home and test, modify, and adjust each recipe for family use, right?"

"Right."

"Well, there you are. If you can reproduce those recipes successfully, then anybody can."

See? Tact all the way.

The reason I chose historical restaurants is that I have a particular affinity for historical settings, and I want to see them preserved. Naturally, nothing pleased me more than to discover that the North Carolina Department of Cultural Resources has set up a section of its organization for the preservation of our structural heritage. This section helps coordinate programs for the rehabilitation of structures that have been designated as historically significant. As you might guess, the criteria for "historically significant" vary considerably. A basic consideration is age; the structure generally must be at least fifty years old. An equally important factor is the building's architectural integrity or uniqueness.

With one exception, all the restaurants in this book meet those requirements. The exception is the Angus Barn. The restaurant was constructed from materials over a hundred years old, and by my criteria, that factor justifies identifying it as historically significant.

Remember how I said I wanted to do all this and stay thin? At the beginning, I didn't know if that was a realistic goal. I found that sometimes I could diet and enjoy myself as much as if I had ordered a heavier meal; other times I threw out the diet and explored the restaurant's more physically inflationary cuisine. How did I emerge? Well, I am still wearing the same dress size I wore fifty restaurants ago.

Comments from my family show that some things have changed, however. My younger daughter said, "Kirsten's mother wants to know if she can have the Coq au Vin recipe." My older daughter said, "Gee, Mama, the kids at school want me to show them how you make puff pastry look like a real fish."

"The Pecan Chicken is the best yet!" my husband told me.

"That's what you said last week about the Veal Madeira Morel," I replied.

"I know, but you just keep topping yourself."

CONTENTS

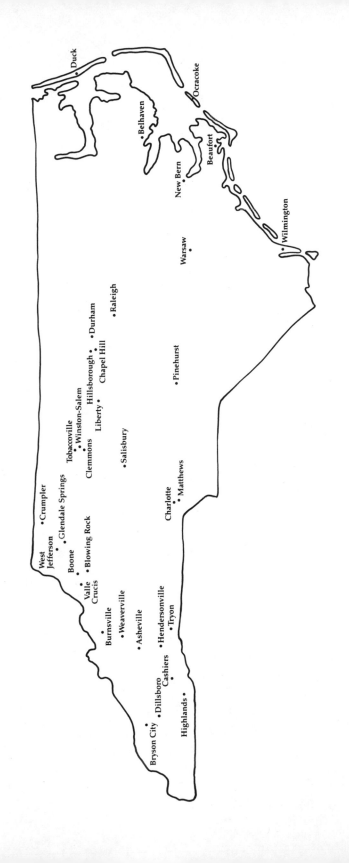

Duck

Ocracoke

Belhaven

Beaufort

New Bern

Wilmington

Warsaw

Raleigh

Durham

Hillsborough • • Chapel Hill
Tobaccoville
• Winston-Salem
Clemmons
Liberty •

• Pinehurst

• Salisbury

• Crumpler
Glendale Springs

• Matthews
Charlotte

West
Jefferson
• Boone • Blowing Rock

Valle
Crucis

Burnsville
• Weaverville
• Asheville
• Hendersonville
• Tryon

Bryson City
• Dillsboro
Cashiers

Highlands •

THE SANDERLING INN
AND RESTAURANT
Duck

THE SANDERLING INN AND RESTAURANT

Two hundred dollars a year was W. G. Partridge's 1874 salary as the first keeper of U. S. Life Saving Station No. 5 at Caffey's Inlet. Both wages and times have changed at the narrowest strip of the Outer Banks. No. 5 was rebuilt in 1899, and it was restored and converted into a handsome restaurant with an adjacent inn in 1982. My husband, John, and I had a terrific view of the ocean from the restaurant's upstairs deck, where we relaxed with Strawberry Daiquiris and appetizers. Our preference was their Hickory-grilled Shrimp, although we did make sizable inroads into their spicy little Clams Casino and their wonderfully fresh and plump Oysters Rockefeller. On a chillier evening the bar, which was formerly the bunk room, might be a cozy choice. Each of the Life Saving Station's six original surfmen was given a small living area with a tiny closet. One surfman's area has been retained to show the modest life of those courageous men.

General Manager Steve Berger pointed out some of the nautical antiques that have been so tastefully incorporated into the décor that they appear to have always been there. Large oars hang on the wall of a downstairs dining room that once housed a huge lifeboat. That dining room is neither fancy nor plain, yet wears a kind of classic simplicity with its pine wainscoting. We began with a salad enlivened by Creamy Vidalia Onion Dressing, which even my onion-hating husband enjoyed. The bread is so good and crunchy with their Currituck Seafood Chowder that I had to limit intake in order to save room for Seafood with Spinach Fettucini, a wholesome blend of scallops, oysters, shrimp, and blue crab nestled in spinach fettucini with a sauce of cream and fresh herbs. You'd expect seafood to be fresh here, and it tasted as if it had been caught while I was dressing for dinner. I wanted to sample the Loin of Lamb in Rosemary Sauce, which John had ordered, but he made it disappear before I had the chance.

The Sanderling has the same strong convictions about dessert that I do. Their homemade Honey-vanilla Ice Cream on top of Sweet Potato Pecan Pie was a first for me, and their fresh Apple and Blueberry pies made with brown sugar and sour cream were equally delicious. A really refreshing Plum Sorbet was the perfect summertime dessert, but John countered that their Triple Chocolate Mousse Cake is a dessert for all seasons. I couldn't argue with that.

After gourmet coffee, we took a leisurely stroll along the beach before turning the key to our luxurious suite. Our bedroom loft overlooked the downstairs living area and the balcony. Inside the closet, we found two terry-cloth robes. Slipping into mine, I thought about those early surfmen who battled the angry waters. Their tiny closets didn't hold clean robes, and I bet they seldom returned from the beach to find a bottle of chilled wine, gourmet snacks, and fruit awaiting them, as we had.

The Sanderling Inn and Restaurant is located five miles north of Duck on N.C. 12. Breakfast is served from 8:00 until 10:00 a.m., lunch from noon until 2:00 p.m., and dinner from 6:00 until 11:00 p.m. daily. Sunday brunch is served from 10:00 a.m. until 3:00 p.m. For reservations call (919) 261-4111.

THE SANDERLING'S
SWEET POTATO PECAN PIE

1 cup chopped pecans	1 teaspoon ground cloves
1 tablespoon butter	1½ teaspoons cinnamon
⅓ cup brown sugar	1 teaspoon ginger
1 8-inch deep-dish pie shell	¼ teaspoon salt
14-ounce can sweet potatoes	2 eggs, beaten
or yams	1½ cups milk
¾ cup brown sugar	

Preheat oven to 450 degrees. Combine pecans, butter, and ⅓ cup brown sugar until mixed. Spread in bottom of pie shell and bake for 10 minutes, turning oven down to 350 degrees. Let cool. Beat sweet potatoes until smooth and add remaining ingredients alternately with milk, beating until smooth. Pour mixture into pie shell and bake for 45 minutes or until a spatula can be inserted an inch from the edge and come out clean. Yields 1 pie.

3

THE SANDERLING'S
SEAFOOD WITH SPINACH FETTUCINI

12 large shrimp, peeled and
  deveined
16 large sea scallops
½ cup shallots, chopped
white pepper to taste
salt to taste

sugar to taste
1 pint heavy cream
24 ounces spinach fettucini
16 oysters, shucked
8 ounces crabmeat

Place shrimp and scallops in a large pot and cover with water. Add shallots, pepper, salt, and sugar. Bring to a boil, then reduce to a simmer until seafood is ¾ cooked. Remove seafood and let stock reduce by half. Add cream and reduce until sauce begins to thicken. Add fettucini, shrimp, scallops, and oysters and toss while cooking on medium-high. When pasta is barely tender, add crabmeat and stir for 30 seconds. Serve with sautéed vegetables of your choice. Serves 4.

THE RIVER FOREST MANOR
Belhaven

THE RIVER FOREST MANOR

As you pass through the Ionic columns into the grandiose entrance hall of The River Forest Manor, try to picture a turn-of-the-century belle who lifts her voluminous skirt and ascends the elaborate stairway to the third-floor ballroom. Such a belle would have been the bride of railroad magnate John Aaron Wilkinson, who spared no expense or imagination to build this majestic mansion for his lady. Wilkinson employed Italian artists who had decorated Biltmore House at Asheville to adorn his ceilings with frescoes and to render the sun's rays in a three-dimensional effect through cleverly positioned beveled glass. The décor is itself a rich dessert that attracted then, as it does today, those who appreciate life's more refined offerings.

The culinary offerings of The River Forest Manor are even more copious now than when the mansion was turned into a restaurant by Axson Smith, Sr., in 1947. Axson, Jr., and his mother, Melba Smith, have continued to expand the epicurean repertoire of the famous smorgasbord, which attracts yacht owners who traverse the Intracoastal Waterway to moor their crafts virtually in the Manor's backyard.

The late Mr. Smith used to love telling of the time he looked out his back door and saw a man washing out his underwear on the deck of his yacht. A closer look revealed the launderer to be none other than Jimmy Cagney. Of course not all guests are that famous, but most yacht owners who wend their way up the Pungo River go there for no better reason than Mrs. Smith's Oyster Fritters, Crabmeat Casserole, and Buttermilk Corn Bread. If those dishes fail to interest you, there are seventy-two delicious alternatives, plus a large selection of wine and beer.

You don't have to own a yacht in order to visit the Manor. Many of the landlubbers who overnight there enjoy the luxury of sleeping in a two-hundred-year-old bed and bathing in a tub built for two! One person sits at each end of the tub. And we thought the Victorian era was dull.

Speaking of bathing, dieters can melt away the smorgasbord in a hot tub outside, or they can carefully choose to dine on fresh vegetables, fruit salads, and broiled seafood. But since that would mean saying no to Strawberry Short-cake, you may feel inclined to follow the Manor's motto: "Eat, drink and be merry for tomorrow you may diet."

The River Forest Manor is located at 600 East Main Street in Belhaven. Dinner is served from 6:00 to 8:30 p.m. Monday through Saturday and from 5:00 until 8:30 p.m. on Sunday. Sunday brunch is served from 9:30 a.m. until 2:00 p.m. The telephone number is (919) 943-2151.

THE RIVER FOREST MANOR'S
MATTIE'S CARAMEL CAKE

1 cup butter
2 cups sugar
4 large eggs
3 scant cups cake flour

3 scant teaspoons baking
   powder
1 cup lukewarm water

Cream butter and sugar. Beat eggs lightly and add to butter and sugar. Sift flour and baking powder together and add to mixture. Add water and beat well. Bake in 3 greased and floured 9-inch pans at 350 degrees until brown and springy, 25 to 30 minutes. Cool and ice with caramel frosting (see recipe below).

THE RIVER FOREST MANOR'S
CARAMEL FROSTING

4 cups light brown sugar
1 cup evaporated milk
¼ teaspoon double-acting
   baking powder

3 tablespoons butter
2 cups chopped nut meats

Boil sugar, milk and baking powder together until mixture comes to a soft boil (238 degrees). Remove from heat and stir in butter. Cool. Add nut meats and beat by hand until mixture is thick enough to spread.

THE RIVER FOREST MANOR'S
PEPPER STEAK

2 pounds sirloin steak
3 large green peppers
2 medium onions
1 cup water chestnuts
3 tablespoons oil
3 tablespoons soy sauce
2 tablespoons brown sugar

2 tablespoons cornstarch
1 teaspoon monosodium
  glutamate
½ cup white wine
½ cup water
3 fresh tomatoes

Cut steak in thin strips across the grain. Chop peppers, onions and water chestnuts. Brown steak quickly in oil and remove from pan. Sauté peppers, onions and water chestnuts. In a separate bowl, mix the soy sauce, brown sugar, cornstarch, monosodium glutamate, wine and water. Combine sauce with the steak and vegetables, and cook 3 to 4 minutes. Serve over hot saffron rice. Garnish with tomato wedges. Serves 4.

THE RIVER FOREST MANOR'S
PAMLICO CRABMEAT CASSEROLE

1 pound fresh crabmeat
1 cup chopped celery
½ cup chopped onions
1 cup mayonnaise
juice of 1 lemon
2 cups seasoned croutons

dash of red hot sauce
salt and pepper
½ cup fine bread crumbs
½ cup Parmesan cheese
¼ cup butter

Combine everything but bread crumbs, butter and cheese; place in a 2-quart casserole dish. Sprinkle with mixture of remaining ingredients. Bake at 350 degrees until casserole bubbles and has browned, 50 to 60 minutes. Serves 10 to 12.

ISLAND INN
Ocracoke

ISLAND INN

The ship, the *Ariosto*, was wrecked on a day when Mrs. Williams' kitchen on Ocracoke held "just a bit of shrimp and a bit of chicken," so she combined them. Her great-grandson embellished this recipe, making it one of the enticements of the Island Inn, but he gave credit for its origin to the inventive woman who needed to feed the survivors of that nineteenth-century disaster.

The resourcefulness of Ocracoke's residents is also evident from the many uses the inn has been given since it was built in 1901. The downstairs was used as a public school until the 1930s, and the crow's nest was officers' quarters during World War II. It was during the navy's stay that the island was so heavily sprayed with insecticides that frogs became extinct. Frogs were imported after the war, and they are now thriving, but their brief absence inspired the extensive frog collection in the Island Inn's lobby. You'll find many delicacies on the inn's menu, but I was assured that frog legs will never be one of them.

I especially enjoyed the appetizer of Oysters with Dill, and when I breakfast at the inn again, I'll have the Oyster Omelet. The Chicken and Shrimp Ariosto is a specialty that must be ordered in advance, but if you don't remember to call ahead, a recommendation is Edna's Crabcakes, which are especially good with a glass of wine or a beer. If you are looking for something a little lighter, investigate the selections listed on the menu as "for the light appetite."

Most visitors to Ocracoke would consider themselves out of luck to be on the island on a cold, rainy day, but that is when the inn is most likely to produce a pot of steaming black-eyed peas and onions. A day such as that would blend in well with the mood of the new décor of the dining room. It is helping the inn regain the look it had when it was first built.

The Island Inn is located on N.C. 12 in Ocracoke. From mid-March through Thanksgiving, breakfast is served from 7:00 until 11:00 a.m. and dinner from 5:00 until 9:00 p.m. seven days a week; lunch is served from 11:20 a.m. until 1:30

p.m. Monday through Saturday. For reservations call (919) 928-7821.

ISLAND INN'S
SHE-CRAB SOUP WITH MARIGOLD

1 cup crabmeat, drained
and flaked
2 cans cream of celery soup
3 cups milk
1 cup half-and-half
1/2 cup butter or margarine
2 boiled eggs, chopped
1/2 teaspoon Old Bay
Seasoning

1/2 teaspoon Worcestershire
sauce
1/4 teaspoon garlic salt
1/4 teaspoon white pepper
1/4 cup dry sherry
chopped marigold leaves

Combine soup, milk, cream, eggs, butter, Old Bay, Worcestershire, garlic and pepper in a large Dutch oven; bring to a boil. Add crabmeat; cook over medium heat, stirring occasionally until heated through. Stir in sherry. Sprinkle each serving with marigold leaves. Yields about 2 quarts.

ISLAND INN'S CHICKEN ELAINE

1 3- to 4-pound chicken
salt and pepper
3 tablespoons ketchup
3 tablespoons brown sugar
2 tablespoon Worcestershire
sauce
2 tablespoons melted butter
2 tablespoons vinegar

1 tablespoon lemon juice
1 small onion, chopped
1 clove garlic, pressed
1 teaspoon salt
1 teaspoon chili powder
1 teaspoon mustard
1/2 teaspoon cayenne

Cut up chicken and season with salt and pepper. Lightly grease inside of brown paper bag; place chicken in bag. Combine remaining ingredients and pour over chicken. Roll up paper bag tightly at both ends. Place in a covered roasting pan. Bake at 350 degrees for 1 hour and 45 minutes. Serves 4.

ISLAND INN'S
SHRIMP AND CHICKEN ARIOSTO

1 3-pound broiler-fryer
1 pound fresh shrimp,
  peeled and deveined
1/2 cup butter
1/2 head cabbage, shredded
1 onion, sliced and
  separated into rings
2 10-ounce cans cream of
  chicken soup, undiluted
1 2-ounce jar diced
  pimientos, undrained

1 teaspoon soy sauce
1/4 teaspoon granulated
  garlic
2 drops liquid smoke
salt and pepper
1/4 cup dry white wine
lettuce leaves or cooked
  brown rice
chopped tomatoes
1/2 cup chopped salted
  peanuts

Boil chicken until tender; remove from bone and flake with a fork. Melt butter in a large Dutch oven; add chicken, shrimp, cabbage and onion. Cook over medium heat until onion is tender. Stir soup, pimientos, soy sauce, garlic and liquid smoke into meat mixture. Season to taste with salt and pepper. Simmer 15 minutes. Stir in wine, and cook 2 additional minutes over low heat. Remove and serve on a lettuce-lined platter or over rice. Garnish with tomatoes and salted peanuts. Serves 6 to 8.

ISLAND INN'S KISS

1/2 ounce Galliano
1 scoop vanilla ice cream

colored sugar crystals

In a champagne glass, place 1/4 ounce Galliano. Add ice cream. Pour another 1/4 ounce Galliano over ice cream. Sprinkle with colored sugar crystals. Keep at room temperature until ice cream begins to melt. Place in freezer until ready to serve. Serves 1.

THE PELICAN RESTAURANT
Ocracoke

THE PELICAN RESTAURANT

The Pelican Restaurant might easily have been named Aunt Fanny's after Fanny Howard. She and her husband, Billy, built this cottage in the 1880s. Since Fanny was known as one of Ocracoke's great cooks, it is most appropriate that her home now serves as one of the finest restaurants on the Outer Banks.

Back when Ocracoke was accessible only by boat, the cost of importing supplies to the island was high. That fact made the inhabitants a resourceful people who shared and took care of each other. Thus, when Billy Howard died in the early part of century, the islanders built him a coffin. When it was completed, however, they discovered that the coffin was too short for its purpose. Unperturbed, Fanny waved the astounded workers aside, climbed into the coffin, and declared that it fit her perfectly. Another coffin was built for her husband, and the practical Fanny kept the first one in her bedroom for seventeen years. Neighbors claim that it became Fanny's favorite leisure-time retreat as well as her final resting place.

When renovating the cottage, workers found an attic full of memorabilia, including a stack of early *Vogue* magazines. Can't you just envision Aunt Fanny getting comfy in her coffin with the latest *Vogue*?

I do believe that Fanny would most heartily approve of the large, screened-in front porch that so carefully has been added to the house. Although I dined in the evening, breakfast on the porch, which is sheltered by weeping willows and hundred-year-old live oaks, must be a very special way to begin the day.

For lunch, burgers and fresh fried fish net high marks. If you prefer something lighter, the Curried Chicken Salad or Marinated Shrimp will help keep you looking fit in your bikini. But dinner is a different story. You could survive wonderfully on the Marinated Steak, but you've really blown it if you don't try the Shrimp in Caper Butter or Coquille St. Jacques. The more excellent is a matter of opinion. In addition, the catch of the day, which is prepared with one of the Pelican's special sauces, is bound to be an improvement over the catch from your local supermarket.

The desserts are outrageous, especially the Chocolate Brandy Cheesecake. Even a sliver will kiss your calorie counter good-bye. There are, however, times and places at which the wisdom of dieting and the wisdom of gourmet dining meet in conflict. The Pelican Restaurant is one of those delightful places.

The Pelican Restaurant is located on N.C. 12 across from the post office in Ocracoke. Breakfast is served from 7:30 to 11:00 a.m., lunch from 11:00 a.m. to 4:00 p.m., and dinner from 5:00 until 9:00 p.m. The restaurant is open from March 1 until November 15. For reservations call (919) 928-7431.

THE PELICAN RESTAURANT'S
SHRIMP IN CAPER BUTTER

40 raw, fresh shrimp, peeled and deveined
3½ cups cooked long-grain white rice
½ cup butter
½ cup diced pimientos
½ cup capers
½ cup diced scallions
1 teaspoon granulated garlic
1 teaspoon whole thyme
¼ cup dry vermouth
¾ cup chicken stock
4 cherry tomatoes
2 tablespoons chopped fresh parsley

Foam butter in large skillet. When bubbles dissipate, add shrimp, pimientos, capers, scallions, garlic and thyme. Cover and cook on high heat until shrimp turn pink. Add vermouth, then chicken stock; cook one minute. Add parsley, rice and tomatoes. Stir well; cover for one minute or until heated through. Serves 4.

THE PELICAN RESTAURANT'S
ZUCCHINI, SOUR CREAM, AND DILL

Vegetable:
4 medium zucchini   3 tablespoons butter

Slice zucchini. Sauté in butter until bright green. Remove and place in a bowl.

Sauce:

3 tablespoons sour cream	1 tablespoon dill weed
2 tablespoons Parmesan cheese	½ teaspoon salt
	dash of granulated garlic

Combine ingredients and pour over sautéed zucchini. Serve at once. Serves 4 to 6.

THE PELICAN RESTAURANT'S MARINATED VEGETABLES

Vegetables:

12 green beans, left long	2 stalks broccoli, cut up
2 medium zucchini, sliced	and stems removed

Steam vegetables separately until crunchy and bright green. Cool.

Dressing:

⅔ cup salad oil	½ cup chopped scallions
½ cup chopped pimientos	¼ teaspoon each rosemary,
⅓ cup red wine vinegar	thyme, granulated garlic,
1 tablespoon capers	paprika, dry mustard,
1 tablespoon Grey Poupon mustard	honey, salt and cayenne

Stir all ingredients together until well blended. Pour over vegetables. Toss and chill 1 hour or longer. Serves 4 to 6.

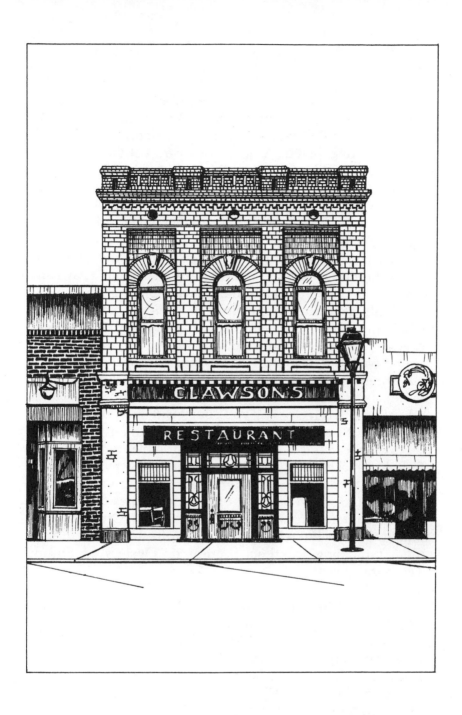

CLAWSON'S 1905 RESTAURANT
Beaufort

CLAWSON'S
1905 RESTAURANT

Clawson's has been in business in the same place since 1905; the delectable difference is that it has been transformed from a grocery and bakery into a restaurant with a saloon. When the building was renovated in 1977, old brick walls, pine flooring and tin ceilings were discovered. A brick courtyard behind the restaurant is where Mr. Clawson did his baking. When he was annoyed by flies, he simply whipped out his gun and shot them off the wall. The former bakery and shooting gallery is now known as Backstreets, an English-style pub complete with darts and games.

After circling back into the unpretentious atmosphere of the restaurant, I ordered the dish that has made Clawson's famous. It is appropriately named the Original Dirigible: it wouldn't take many to transform your appearance into that of a blimp. The Dirigible is a huge baked potato stuffed with cheeses, seafood, sour cream, and other taste treats that respond well to a glass of chablis or a beer from their extensive assortment. For your benefit (which turned out also to be mine), I sampled the Clam Chowder. I was unsuccessful at wheedling that recipe for you, but I did succeed in getting their Mud Pie, which adds a nice dessert to any meal.

At dinner you can still have the Dirigible, but Back Ribs, Buffalo Chicken Wings and fresh seafood always claim center stage. If you prefer a lighter meal in the summer, you can order their Seafood Salad or one of their pasta dishes. During the winter, you can think of their French Onion Soup or a Ribeye Steak, but when I'm this near fresh seafood in summer, I'm going for their Scampi or Oysters or Shrimp Tempura.

Clawson's 1905 Restaurant is located at 429 Front Street in Beaufort. During the high season, meals are served from 11:30 a.m. until 9:30 p.m. Monday through Saturday; dinner is served on Sunday. During the off-season, lunch is served from 11:30 a.m. until 2:00 p.m. and dinner is served from 6:00 until 9:00 p.m. Monday through Saturday. The telephone number is (919) 728-2133.

CLAWSON'S ORIGINAL DIRIGIBLE

1 1-pound potato
1 tablespoon butter
1 tablespoon chopped
  onion
1 tablespoon chopped green
  pepper
1/8 cup diced ham
1/8 cup diced turkey

1/8 cup shredded provolone
  cheese
1/8 cup shredded cheddar
  cheese
1/4 cup sour cream
pinch of chives
2 slices cooked bacon,
  crumbled

Bake potato at 400 degrees for 1 hour or until done. Split open and rake with fork. Work in butter, onion and pepper; work in diced ham, turkey and cheeses. Close potato and heat until cheese melts. Remove and top with sour cream, chives, and bacon. For a seafood Dirigible, substitute cooked, minced crab and shrimp for ham and turkey. Serves 1.

CLAWSON'S MUD PIE

1-pound bag Oreo cookies
1/2 cup chocolate syrup
1/2 gallon heavenly hash ice
  cream, softened
1 cup whipping cream

1/2 cup almond slivers
6 to 8 maraschino cherries
6 tablespoons chocolate
  syrup

Crush cookies in a food processor. Mix 2/3 pound of cookies with 1/2 cup of chocolate syrup. Press mixture onto bottom and sides of a 9- or 10-inch deep-dish pie pan. Scoop ice cream into crust with a large spoon. Press ice cream down with spoon. Sprinkle remaining 1/3 of a pound of cookies over top and wrap with aluminum foil. Place in freezer overnight or for several hours until pie sets. When ready to serve, whip cream until peaks form. Remove pie, cut into wedges and top each wedge with whipped cream, almonds and a maraschino cherry. Drizzle six tablespoons of chocolate syrup over top. Yields 1 pie.

CLAWSON'S SHRIMP POCKET SANDWICHES

1 pound baby shrimp,
  peeled and steamed
1 stalk celery, chopped fine
2/3 cup mayonnaise
2 to 3 teaspoons Cavenders
  Greek Seasoning
juice of 1/4 lemon

dash of Tabasco
6 Pita breads
1/2 cup shredded lettuce
12 slices tomato
12 slices cucumber
1/2 cup alfalfa sprouts

Combine shrimp, celery, mayonnaise, seasoning, lemon juice and Tabasco and mix well. Spread mixture into Pita pockets. Stuff with lettuce, 2 slices of tomato and 2 slices of cucumber each. Top with alfalfa sprouts. Serves 6.

POPLAR GROVE PLANTATION
Wilmington

POPLAR GROVE PLANTATION

Poplar Grove Plantation was on the list of restaurants in historical settings that was given to me by the North Carolina Department of Cultural Resources, so why no one knew where it was located remains a mystery to this day.

Having finished the restaurants in Wilmington, I was on my way out of town, took a wrong turn, and "found" Poplar Grove Plantation. The caretaker, Mr. Norris, was just leaving when I arrived and explained my interest in the restaurant. He gallantly gave me a personally guided tour through one of the most beautifully restored plantation homes that I have ever visited. He left out no detail, not even the cypress balcony porches that slant to allow the rain to drain naturally.

Historians have recorded that this was the state's first peanut-producing plantation, purchased in 1795 by James Foy, Jr., the son of a revolutionary war hero. It wasn't until 1850 that the present house, an immense two-story Greek Revival frame house, was built by Joseph M. Foy. He was the son of James Foy, Jr., and is renowned as a pioneering champion of human rights. I am told that examples of his progressive beliefs in equality are demonstrated today in the costumed "living dramas" that are held at the house. The dramas take place in the rooms where similar conversations are believed to have been held between Foy and his slaves. Grievances were heard, discussed, and acted upon accordingly, which was an unprecedented arrangement during that era.

It appears that other generations of the Foys were able to extend their philosophy of human rights to include women. This is evident from the fact that Aunt Nora, who married James T. Foy and came to the plantation in 1871, later became the postmistress. Aunt Nora died in 1923, and I am told that her spirit continues to be felt from time to time. It is said that at night she can be heard pacing upstairs in what was her bedroom. And on the night of the annual candlelight tour, a glow has been seen at Aunt Nora's window long after the guests departed and all the candles were extinguished.

It was too late to dine on my first visit, so I returned later for a delicious lunch. The restaurant's fare is prepared by recipes that have been handed down from family heads and old slave cooks. I have tested the recipes that have been so generously shared with me, however. If the Coconut Pie, originated by Aunt Betty, mistress of the plantation at the turn of the century, is any indication of the present dining room's quality, my sweet tooth would give it a high mark. My whole family felt that the Chicken Fantastic is appropriately named. The manager of Poplar Grove Plantation, Nancy Simon, recommended the stuffed tomatoes or a plate of fruit and cottage cheese for dieters.

The dining room also serves Sunday dinners, which have waiting lines that extend up the driveway, another good indication of the food's quality. The Christmas menu also sounds very special. It features either ham, turkey, or roast pork, with pineapple sweet potatoes, pecan pie, cranberry Waldorf salad, and a glass of house wine, all for less money than I can prepare a Christmas meal myself. At any time of the year, you have the privilege of ordering wines that come from neighboring Duplin County.

The plantation's azalea blossoms were at their peak when I visited, but I'd like to return at Christmas to see for myself the burning candle in Aunt Nora's window. I would like to try to initiate some kind of communication with her—but perhaps she has already communicated with me. After all, I, who am a seasoned traveler, did take the "wrong" road that led me directly to Poplar Grove Plantation. Isn't that curious?

Poplar Grove Plantation is located at Scott's Hill, nine miles north of Wilmington on U.S. 17. Lunch is served from 11:30 a.m. to 2:30 p.m. Monday through Saturday. Dinner is served from 6:00 until 8:00 p.m. Tuesday through Saturday. Sunday brunch is served from 11:00 a.m. to 2:30 p.m. For reservations call (919) 686-9503.

POPLAR GROVE PLANTATION'S
AUNT BETTY'S COCONUT PIE

2 tablespoons margarine,
softened
1½ cups sugar
1½ cups evaporated milk
1½ cups flake coconut

3 eggs, beaten
1 tablespoon flour or
cornstarch
1 teaspoon vanilla
1 9-inch pie shell, unbaked

Cream sugar and margarine. Mix remaining ingredients, pour into pie shell and bake at 350 degrees for 30 minutes.

POPLAR GROVE PLANTATION'S
CHICKEN FANTASTIC

1 3- to 4-pound chicken,
cooked
¼ cup butter
3 tablespoons chopped
onion
3 teaspoons chopped
pimientos
1 10-ounce package frozen
French-cut green beans,
thawed

1 8-ounce can water
chestnuts, chopped
1 6-ounce package wild
rice, cooked
½ cup mayonnaise
1 10-ounce can cream of
celery soup

Pull chicken from the bones and tear into bite-size pieces. Melt butter in a skillet and sauté onion until transparent. Brown chicken, adding more butter if needed. Grease a casserole dish and combine all ingredients. Bake in a pre-heated 350-degree oven for 40 minutes. Serves 8.

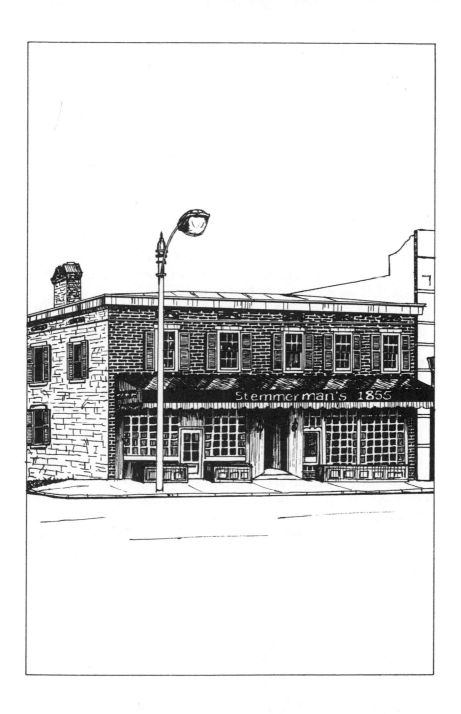

STEMMERMAN'S 1855
Wilmington

STEMMERMAN'S
1855

Inevitably, the city of Wilmington discovers another tunnel whenever it digs underground near the Cape Fear River. Each discovery adds to the knowledge of the intricate network of tunnels that once functioned as a conduit for the blockade runners during the Civil War.

Charles Stemmerman ran a seemingly innocent grocery store on Front Street, but his downstairs warehouse served a dangerous function. Even today as you pass the brick and ballast-stone walls at the last curve of the stairway, you can see where a large tunnel was sealed over. Moving my hand over the seal, I thought of the people who had crept through that tunnel to the harbor exit, and of the smuggled munitions that were stored in that warehouse.

I closed my eyes as I sat in a high wooden booth, and scenes of courage and heroism flickered through my mind. I wondered if the rather exorbitant $10,500 Stemmerman had paid for is grocery store operation in 1855 had been recouped by his trafficking in military supplies.

My dinner companion brought me back to reality when our wonderful appetizer of bacon and oysters, called Angels on Horseback, arrived. It was followed by the restaurant's famous and delicious Flounder Marguery and the Sour Cream Chicken. We were certainly not counting calories that night, as I had the day before at lunch, when I had the Seafood Salad on the upstairs veranda called the Cafe Upstairs.

The Cafe Upstairs, with its tranquilizing view of the river, is adjacent to the original grocery area, which has been transformed into an attractive dining room with exposed brick and stained glass windows. The view set me to wonder if the same boats transporting supplies to the Confederacy could have hidden runaway slaves. Stranger tales have been told. This is what I really appreciate about Stemmerman's—not only is it satisfying to your taste buds, but its rich history stimulates your imagination.

Stemmerman's 1855 is located at 138 South Front Street in

Wilmington. Lunch is served Monday through Saturday from 11:30 a.m. to 3:00 p.m., and dinner from 5:00 to 10:00 p.m. Stemmerman's 1855 also operates the Cafe Upstairs, which is open from 9:00 a.m. until 4:00 p.m. seven days a week. For reservations call (919) 763-7776.

STEMMERMAN'S ANGELS ON HORSEBACK

12 slices bacon
12 oysters
12 toothpicks
chopped parsley

paprika
1/2 cup sour cream
2 tablespoons horseradish

Fry bacon until half-done. Remove from skillet and lay out on a cookie sheet. Place one oyster on center of bacon and sprinkle with parsley and paprika. Roll bacon over oyster and secure with a toothpick. Bake at 350 degrees until bacon crisps. Meanwhile, mix sour cream and horseradish together. When bacon and oysters are done, spoon sauce over them. Serves 4.

STEMMERMAN'S SOUR CREAM CHICKEN

5 1/2-pound chicken breasts
1 pint sour cream
1/2 cup lemon juice
1 ounce medium-dry sherry
3 cloves garlic, minced

1 tablespoon celery salt
1/2 tablespoon salt
1/4 teaspoon paprika
1/4 teaspoon pepper
1 cup bread crumbs

Combine sour cream, lemon juice, sherry, garlic, celery salt, salt, paprika and pepper in a bowl and mix thoroughly. Skin chicken breasts and place in marinade; refrigerate for at least 24 hours. When ready to cook, spread chicken breasts flat on a greased sheet and sprinkle tops with bread crumbs to cover. Bake at 350 degrees for 10 to 12 minutes or until the meat is firm. Place each breast on a bed of herbed long-grain and wild rice. Serves 5.

STEMMERMAN'S FLOUNDER MARGUERY

8 ½-pound flounder filets
¼ pound shrimp, split
  lengthwise
1 cup oysters with liquor
¼ cup butter
⅓ cup flour
½ pound mushrooms,
  sliced
1 teaspoon butter

1¾ cups half-and-half
3 tablespoons lemon juice
5 tablespoons sherry
½ teaspoon paprika
¼ teaspoon salt
¼ teaspoon white pepper
more salt and pepper to
  taste

Melt butter in a saucepan; stir in flour, making a roux, until the flour takes on a nutty aroma. Do not brown. In a separate saucepan sauté the mushrooms in the teaspoon of butter. To the roux add the half-and-half, lemon juice, sherry, paprika, salt and pepper, shrimp and oysters and liquor; heat to the boiling point, stirring with wire whisk to remove lumps. Add the mushrooms, and more salt and pepper to taste; simmer a few more minutes while the flavors combine. As sauce simmers, broil flounder until flaky. Remove from broiler and cover with sauce. Serves 8.

HARVEY HOUSE RESTAURANT
New Bern

HARVEY HOUSE RESTAURANT

When you arrive at Harvey House, which is commandingly positioned on the Trent River, turn your memory back to 1791. Think of old John Harvey directing shipments of cargo from the warehouse inside his home onto the merchant ships anchored below. History reports that this wealthy plantation owner from Shropshire, England, owned thirty slaves. It was, no doubt, the slaves who hauled those bales of barley and tobacco from the plantation across town to the store and warehouse, and from there onto the ships.

Today, as you enter Harvey House, you are still greeted by the hand-carved rosewood staircase that has been authentically restored by Bob and Coral Clark. Each of the six dining rooms has been wallpapered and decorated in the Federal style to preserve the atmosphere of the era in which the house was built. Harvey House's original kitchen, which now serves as the cocktail lounge, is a cozy setting, with its exposed brick and its handsome brass and teak bar.

To keep up with the trend of our times, the Clarks have designated smoking and nonsmoking dining rooms for their guests' comfort. They feel that the restaurant and bar fit in well with the vigorous spirit of John Harvey, who died at the age of seventy-four, shortly after the birth of a daughter.

You didn't think I'd forget about the food, did you? *Southern Living* magazine described Harvey House's continental menu as having "touches of the lighter nouvelle cuisine."

The chef specializes in preparing fresh game fish purchased locally. My favorite entrée is Veal Madeira Morel, a special dinner for a special night out. Close competition comes from the Tryon Palace Shrimp, a wonderful concoction of jumbo shrimp stuffed with crab imperial and covered with Canadian bacon.

Harvey House Restaurant is located at 221 Tryon Palace Drive in New Bern. Lunch is served from 11:30 a.m. until 2:30 p.m. Tuesday through Friday, with Sunday brunch also from 11:30 a.m. until 2:30 p.m. Dinner is served from 5:30 until 9:30 p.m. Tuesday through Sunday. The lounge opens at 5:00 p.m. For reservations call (919) 638-3205.

HARVEY HOUSE'S
VEAL MADEIRA MOREL

Brown sauce:

3 tablespoons butter
¼ cup plain flour
4 cups beef stock or beef
  broth, homemade or
  commercial
1 cup chopped tomatoes or
  ¾ cup tomato paste
2 teaspoons vegetable oil

1 medium carrot, chopped
1 medium onion, chopped
1 to 2 stalks celery,
  chopped
pinch of thyme
1 bay leaf, crushed
2 tablespoons sherry

Melt 2 tablespoons of the butter in a large saucepan; blend in the flour to make a smooth paste. Cook until brown. Add beef stock or broth gradually, stirring until smooth. Add tomatoes or tomato paste, stirring until smooth. In a separate pan, heat remaining tablespoon of butter with oil; stir in carrots, onions and celery, sautéing until tender. Stir in thyme, bay leaf and sherry. Add this mixture to beef stock mixture and simmer until sauce is reduced by half, stirring occasionally. Strain through a fine sieve. Yields about 2½ cups. Brown sauce is the cornerstone of many fine sauces. Store what is not needed immediately in airtight containers and freeze.

Veal:

2 to 3 tablespoons butter
½ pound veal
2 tablespoons plain flour
salt and pepper to taste
3 to 4 tablespoons morel
  mushrooms (see note)

6 tablespoons Madeira
3 tablespoons brandy
½ cup brown sauce
1 tablespoon or more heavy
  whipping cream

Melt butter in sauté pan. Pound veal thin and dust with flour. Add salt and pepper. Sauté veal for approximately 30 seconds on one side. Turn veal over and add morels, Madeira and brandy. Quickly light match and ignite alcohol in pan and let it burn off. Stir in ½ cup brown sauce and simmer for 10 seconds. Add cream and swirl with spoon to blend. Serve on warmed plates and garnish with additional morels. Serves 2.

Note: If morels are unavailable, use shitake mushrooms, which may be found at health food stores or specialty grocery stores. If regular mushrooms are used sauté or blanch until tender before adding.

HARVEY HOUSE'S CRAB IMPERIAL

Crab mixture:

½ green bell pepper, diced
½ red pepper, diced
4 tablespoons capers
2 tablespoons Dijon
  mustard
½ teaspoon seafood
  seasoning

dash of Worcestershire
  sauce
dash of lemon juice
6 tablespoons mayonnaise
1 pound back fin crabmeat

Lightly grease a 1- to 1½-quart casserole or 6 ramekin dishes. Combine all ingredients except crab and mix thoroughly. Fold in crabmeat gently in order not to break it down. Bake in a preheated 350-degree oven for 20 minutes.

Imperial sauce:

3 egg yolks
dash of Worcestershire
  sauce

dash of lemon juice
4 tablespoon mayonnaise

Beat egg yolks in a small bowl. Add Worcestershire sauce, lemon juice and mayonnaise, stirring until smooth. Spoon 2 or 3 tablespoons of sauce over crab mixture. Place under broiler for a few minutes to brown. Serves 6.

HENDERSON HOUSE
New Bern

HENDERSON HOUSE

Usually a restaurant excels in either cuisine, atmosphere, décor or history, but at Henderson House each category rivals the others. The house is a three-story brick structure believed to have been built in the 1790s as a wedding gift from Dr. Thomas Haslen, a member of Governor William Tryon's Royal Council, for his daughter Sarah.

When I first visited, the top floor housed a toy shop. The former owners sought all kinds of reasons to explain why the dolls and toys stored on shelves at closing time were found on the floor on more than one morning, as if a child had been playing with them. Only after researching the history of the house did they discover that a nine-year-old boy died there and that his mother died some years later. She is a very peaceful spirit, but apparently the little boy can't resist a child's temptations from time to time. The top floor is now an impressive art gallery, featuring works by Robert Weaver, the father of owner and chef Matthew Weaver.

The dining rooms, with Federal mantels and handmade moldings, have been decorated to the tastes of the eighteenth century. The eleven-and-a-half-foot ceilings are covered in a light moiré silk, and one of the rooms contains its original floor-to-ceiling gold-leaf mirror. The Federal-style décor has been carried even to the waitresses' costumes with their long aprons.

The day I lunched at Henderson House was a bit nippy, so I ordered a pot of tea. My teapot was kept hot with an English tea cozy, suggesting a splendid attention to detail. The Epicurean Sandwich is a meal in itself, with ham and turkey baked under a delicate mushroom sauce. I also sampled the Chicken Salad, which was the best I'd ever tasted. It had large chunks of chicken in a light sauce that hinted of herbs. Another little marvel is broiled crabmeat and cheese, which is laced with spices and served on an English muffin. The homemade muffins are another treat. For dessert I had a scrumptious meringue shell topped with ice cream and chocolate sauce.

For evening fare I would choose Tournedos de Boeuf with Béarnaise sauce or their Coquille St. Jacques. The wine list ranges from inexpensive vintage wines to excellent champagnes.

Henderson House boasts a Mobil three-star rating and has received the Silver Spoon Award for five years running. It is listed on the National Register of Historic Places as the Hatch-Washington House, and its distinguished guests have run the gamut from the Sheik of Kuwait to actor Don Johnson. Even the most finicky connoisseur would be hard-pressed to register a complaint against this restaurant, which strives to make every customer as comfortable as possible.

Henderson House is located at 216 Pollock Street in New Bern. Lunch is served from 11:30 a.m. until 2:00 p.m. and dinner is served from 6:00 until 9:00 p.m. Wednesday through Saturday. The restaurant welcomes private parties by prior arrangement. For reservations call (919) 637-4784.

HENDERSON HOUSE'S
SOUR CREAM MUFFINS

½ cup sweet unsalted
   butter
1½ cups sugar
½ teaspoon salt
1½ cups sour cream
4 eggs, beaten

½ teaspoon vanilla
⅔ cup all-purpose flour,
   sifted
1 teaspoon baking soda
24 muffin or cupcake
   liners, oiled

Cream butter, sugar and salt with an electric mixer. Beat in sour cream until well mixed. Beat in eggs and vanilla until well mixed. Slowly fold in flour and baking soda, mixing until incorporated. Place liners in lightly greased muffin tins and spoon in mixture until ⅔ full. Bake in a preheated 300-degree oven for 20 minutes or until brown. Yields 24 muffins.

HENDERSON HOUSE'S COLD PEACH SOUP

3 cups peaches and juice   1 cup sour cream or yogurt
(fresh, frozen, or canned)   ½ teaspoon almond extract

Place skinned and chopped peaches with other ingredients into a blender and blend until frothy. Serve chilled.
Will keep a day or so. Serves 4.

Excellent for sufferers of flu or sore throat, or on a hot day.

THE COUNTRY SQUIRE
Warsaw

THE COUNTRY SQUIRE

The moment I stepped out of the rain and into the dim torch-lit, brick-floored hearth room at The Country Squire, I thought, "What a wonderful place for a rendezvous." A blazing fire welcomed my chilled bones as the fragrance of apples in a barrel greeted my nostrils. I was seated in a country, cozy log cabin room that has a big fat tree growing through the center of it. The tree has a cushioned bench surrounding its trunk.

You can't imagine how good the Squire's Clam Chowder tasted on that chilly day. Being as faithful to my diet as possible, I also had an Asparagus Salad with a pot of hot English tea. The restaurant now serves alcoholic beverages including wine from the nearby Duplin winery.

Although the Squire does a fantastic Crab Louise and Shrimp Fritchey for dinner, it is best known for its "mood cooking with an Asian accent." The Korean Barbecued Beef and Kailua Steak are absolutely outstanding. Also not to be missed is the Squire's Brown Rice. Any of the broiled steaks and seafood should get your diet's okay, but if you request in advance, the Squire can accommodate most any requirements.

After touring the Squire's various dining rooms, all of which have an English flavor, I decided that the Baronial Hall was most impressive. It features its original wide plank floors, tables suspended from the ceiling with heavy chains, and the portrait of Baron Gilbert De Clair. Although no actual testing was done when the late parapsychologist from Duke University, Dr. J. B. Rhine, visited the Squire, he is said to have believed that the Baronial Hall was inhabited by spirits. If so, I don't blame them for not wanting to leave this warm and festive habitat. The Squire's Vintage Inn, an adjoining twelve-room motel, continues the mood of the restaurant and allows for a pleasant weekend getaway.

Not only is the Squire's interior inviting, but many of the rooms' diamond-shaped windows look out on beautiful gardens. Paths wind their way among tall pine and oak trees where the design has disturbed as little of nature as possible.

The Country Squire is located on N.C. 24, five miles east of Warsaw. Continental breakfast is provided for guests of The Squire's Vintage Inn. The restaurant serves lunch from 11:30 a.m. until 2:00 p.m. Monday through Friday and from noon until 2:00 p.m. on Sunday. Dinner is served from 5:30 until 10:00 p.m. Sunday through Thursday, and from 5:30 until 11:00 p.m. on Friday and Saturday. For reservations call (919) 296-1727.

THE COUNTRY SQUIRE'S
SWEET AND SOUR SAUCE

juice of two lemons
1 small green pepper,
    chopped
½ to ¾ cup water

¾ cup light brown sugar
¾ tablespoon or more
    cornstarch
1 teaspoon vinegar

Combine all ingredients in a saucepan and cook until sauce is thick and green pepper is tender.

THE COUNTRY SQUIRE'S
KAILUA STEAK

3 ribeye steaks
⅜ cup soy sauce
2 teaspoons sesame oil
½ clove garlic, minced
2¼ teaspoons sugar
1 teaspoon chopped fresh
    chives or onion
about 6 scallions

1 egg
1 teaspoon any type oil
⅓ cup milk
3 tablespoons flour
sesame seeds
oil for deep frying
seedless grapes or
    mandarin oranges

Cut steaks into ¼-inch strips. Mix soy sauce, sesame oil, garlic, sugar and chives in a 2-cup container and add water to fill. Cover steak with mixture and marinate in refrigerator for 24 hours. Alternate strips of meat and scallions between two skewers, piercing each onion and strip of meat on both ends. Make a batter of egg, 1 teaspoon oil, milk and flour.

Dip beef and onion in batter, then roll in sesame seeds to coat. Deep fry until light brown. Remove skewers, top with grapes or orange slices, and serve with sweet and sour sauce (see recipe below). Serves 4.

THE COUNTRY SQUIRE'S
BARBECUED SPARERIBS

5 to 6 pounds lean
  spareribs
2½ ounces Heinz 57 Sauce
2½ ounces Worcestershire
  sauce
2½ ounces A-1 Steak Sauce
1½ cups catsup
1 cup cider vinegar

2 cups water
¾ cup sugar
1 teaspoon Tabasco
horseradish
2 to 3 tablespoons sesame
  seeds, browned

Cut ribs into 2-rib sections and place in a large flat pan in a 400-degree oven for 10 minutes. Turn ribs over and cook for about 5 additional minutes. Reduce heat to 275 degrees. Combine Heinz 57 Sauce, Worcestershire sauce, A-1 Steak Sauce, catsup, vinegar, water, sugar and Tabasco in a medium-size bowl. Stir until well mixed. Drain fat from ribs and blot with a paper towel. Pour 3 to 4 cups of barbecue sauce over ribs and return to oven. Cover and cook for 1 to 1½ hours until ribs are tender, turning ribs occasionally. Place ribs on a charcoal grill for flavor. Serve with horseradish and browned sesame seeds. Serves 4 to 5.

THE MANOR INN
Pinehurst

THE MANOR INN

I f you happen to be out bicycling in Pinehurst and find yourself in the mood for refreshment, The Manor Inn is one of the few places where you can expect your bicycle to be parked by the doorman. That was the discovery four young women made one Mother's Day. Though it was a busy day for the Manor, none of the unusual amenities were amiss.

Upon your arrival at this Southern landscaped filigree of dogwoods, you'll notice that the 1923 white stucco structure is accented by an abundance of red geraniums. They spill out of the window boxes from early spring through the fall. It is during these seasons that the rockers lining the front porch offer a beguiling invitation to sit and sip the Manor's "iced tea." The drink is an interesting alcoholic concoction that does not include tea. That minor infraction has not deterred the drink's popularity in the least.

Inside the cozy interior are a number of dining options to suit one's choice of atmosphere or the time of day. I enjoyed the sun porch and, in particular, my escargots, an ingenious appetizer-sandwich consisting of mushroom-stuffed snails nestled inside a Kaiser roll.

Dinner at the Manor usually takes on a somewhat grander significance, with intricate ice carvings, silver champagne coolers, and six courses selected from a rotating menu. The cuisine is basically continental in style, with Oysters Rockefeller and Stuffed Shrimp commanding the most attention for appetizers. The entrées are split fairly evenly between classic French dishes and more standard fare as Filet Mignon, Fried Chicken, and Baked Ham. Desserts are similar in choice, ranging from Lemon Soufflé to Apple Pie

If you are vacationing at the Manor, then you should also try the Yorkshire Popovers for breakfast. After any meal you'll find that there is such a variety of recreation possibilities that you can work off any superfluous calories by swimming, golf, tennis or the riding club's offering of tree-lined horse trails. Then you can come back for another sumptuous meal or maybe just collapse on the front porch with a glass of "iced tea."

The Manor is located on Magnolia Road in Pinehurst. It is open throughout the year. Breakfast is served from 7:00 to 9:00 a.m., lunch from 11:30 a.m. to 1:30 p.m., and dinner from 6:30 to 9:00 p.m. For reservations call (919) 295-2700.

THE MANOR INN'S
BAKED SMOKED HAM IN RYE DOUGH

1 smoked ham	mustard to coat ham
½ cup brown sugar	rye bread dough (recipe
1 small can crushed	follows)
pineapple	

Coat ham with a layer each of mustard, brown sugar and drained pineapple. Roll out dough and wrap around ham. Bake at 350 degrees for 2 hours. Some say you should throw the ham away and eat the rye bread. Five-pound ham serves 10 to 12.

THE MANOR INN'S RYE BREAD

1 pint water, boiling	2 tablespoons dry active
2 tablespoons butter	yeast
2 tablespoons sugar	7 cups unbleached white
1½ teaspoons salt	flour
cold water	2½ cups rye flour

Combine boiling water, butter, sugar and salt in a mixing bowl. Stir until butter melts; then add cold water and stir until mixture is lukewarm. Stir in yeast and let sit 5 minutes. Stir in 3 cups white flour and all the rye. Beat vigorously until smooth. Work in enough remaining flour to make a stiff dough. Then turn out onto a floured board and knead until smooth and satiny. Place dough in a greased bowl, oil the top of the dough, cover with a cloth, and place in a warm spot to rise. Dough should double in bulk. Punch down; shape half into a loaf to bake and wrap the remainder around the ham. After loaf has risen a second time, put in greased 9- by 5- by 3-inch covered loaf pan, then bake at 350 degrees for about an hour.

THE MANOR INN'S
FRIED STUFFED SHRIMP

12 to 15 large shrimp,
  butterflied
1 can water chestnuts
4 ounces prosciutto ham

2 to 3 eggs
flour for dredging
oil for frying

Chop 3 to 4 shrimp and water chestnuts into paste. Spread this mixture on remainder of shrimp. Cover with prosciutto ham. Dip in beaten egg and dredge in flour. Let dry on rack and slide into deep fat at 375 degrees and cook until golden brown. Serve with sweet and sour sauce. (see Index). Serves 4 to 6.

THE MANOR INN'S ICED TEA

1 ounce gin
1 ounce rum
1½ ounces whiskey sour
  mix

½ ounce Triple Sec
1 ounce vodka
Coca-Cola
ice

Pour liquors and whiskey sour mix into an 8-ounce glass and shake. Fill glass with Coke and ice. Stir. Serves 1.

PINE CREST INN
Pinehurst

PINE CREST INN

As you drive through the towering pines and varied, lush plantings that characterize the Pinehurst of today, it is hard to imagine that this golfer's utopia was created out of a barren wilderness. The tract was nothing but leveled tree stumps when James G. Tufts bought it in 1895 and hired landscape architect Frederick Law Olmstead to design a resort for convalescents. If anyone could create a pleasant spot out of that land it was Olmstead, who had designed New York City's Central Park and the gardens of Biltmore House in Asheville.

Tufts led Pinehurst in a new direction entirely when he found his healthier patrons disturbing the cattle in his fields by hitting little white balls with clubs. Going against the common belief that golf was a passing fancy, Tufts built a nine-hole course. In 1900 Scottish golf pro Donald Ross arrived at Pinehurst and began designing more courses. The success of golf at Pinehurst earned international reputations for both Ross and the resort.

Ross eventually invested some of his earnings at Pinehurst by buying the 1913 Pine Crest Inn. He endowed the inn with a comfortable, sporty atmosphere that has remained intact since golfer Bob Barrett purchased Pine Crest in 1961. The inn has been featured in *Ford Times* magazine.

I found that visiting the inn today is like slipping on an old shoe. There are no signs reading "No stuffy people allowed," because that isn't necessary. The stuffies couldn't withstand the inn's hearty camaraderie. I don't think it is possible to remain a stranger at Pine Crest for more than thirty minutes; some guest has either dragged you over to the bar and introduced you to everyone, or you're in a sing-along around the piano.

After a long trip I was easily persuaded to try a Transfusion, an unlikely drink of vodka, Gatorade and grape juice. It slipped down remarkably easily in the company of the inn's voluptuous little Gouda Puffs.

Luckily my group realized in time that we were about to miss dinner, so we settled down in the main dining room, which is decorated with cheerful wallpaper and crystal chandeliers. The cuisine at Pine Crest can best be described as pure Americana. The chef, Carl Jackson, has been with the inn for fifty-four years. He specializes in "sincere" cooking, such as fresh-squeezed orange juice for breakfast and "scratch" bran muffins, not to mention the best clam chowder I've had in this state.

Our meal began with a fresh Crabmeat Cocktail and a gentle Bordeaux from the Lichine vineyards. The wine was the exact prescription for my tremendous Filet Mignon served with tiny boiled potatoes, green beans al dente, and the tastiest fried zucchini to be found anywhere. I can hardly believe that I found room for my Blueberry Cream Pie, which was served with a Cabernet. Then, because someone insisted that we finish the meal with a smooth drink called the Afterglow, we did. After two of those, you do glow!

The Pine Crest Inn offers a convivial atmosphere that lures you to sink down in one of the overstuffed chairs beside the fire and "set and joke a spell" while the world struggles along without you.

The Pine Crest Inn is located on Dogwood Road in Pinehurst. Breakfast is served from 7:00 to 9:00 a.m., and dinner from 7:00 to 9:00 p.m. For reservations call (919) 295-6121.

PINE CREST INN'S SIX WEEKS MUFFINS

3 cups Bran Buds	2 cups buttermilk
1¼ cups boiling water	2½ cups all-purpose flour
2 beaten eggs	2½ teaspoons soda
1½ cups sugar	1 teaspoon salt
½ cup vegetable oil	1 teaspoon cinnamon

Pour water over bran and set aside. In electric mixer beat eggs; add sugar, oil and buttermilk one at a time, mixing thoroughly. Scrape sides with rubber spatula to incorporate ingredients. Pour into greased muffin tins, filling each cup a little more than half full. Bake at 375 degrees for about 30 minutes. For miniature tins, bake about 12 minutes. Yields 24 large muffins.

PINE CREST INN'S GOUDA PUFFS

1 ½-pound wheel Gouda
cheese
1 package Pepperidge Farm
crescent rolls

2 teaspoons caraway seeds
1 egg white

Split Gouda horizontally to make two thinner rounds. Divide crescent roll dough into squares and arrange around each circle of Gouda. Tuck pastry securely in place and sprinkle with caraway seeds. Place on greased cookie sheet with seam side down. Brush with egg white. Bake at 350 degrees for 15 to 25 minutes. Cut into bite-sized wedges and serve hot. Serves 4.

PINE CREST INN'S
SPINACH AND MUSHROOM SALAD

1 pound fresh spinach
½ pound fresh mushrooms,
stemmed
2 ripe avocadoes
Naturally Fresh Poppy Seed
Dressing

¼ cup olive oil
⅓ package dry Ranch Herb
Dressing

Wash spinach; stem and tear into bite-sized pieces. Place in plastic bag in refrigerator to crispen. Marinate mushrooms in Poppy Seed Dressing for an hour. Combine olive oil with herb dressing. Peel and slice avocadoes. Toss together spinach, herb dressing, mushrooms and avocadoes. Serves 6.

PINE CREST INN'S AFTERGLOW

1 ounce vodka
1 ounce Grand Marnier
1 ounce Bailey's Irish
Cream

1 ounce Kahlua
2 ounces heavy cream
ice

Combine all ingredients in blender and blend until frothy. Serves 2.

THE ANGUS BARN
Raleigh

THE ANGUS BARN I f grassroots America of the early part of the century were described, mention would be made of old country barns, Mom churning butter, Dad bringing in logs, children stringing popcorn at Christmas, and the unmistakable aroma of a baking pie greeting you at the kitchen door. These are some of the things that today's children read about but old-timers remember.

The feelings of an earlier time can be rekindled at the Angus Barn. This is partly because the building is an assemblage of ancient barns and dwellings. In the Angus Tavern area, for instance, sturdy old log beams blend with the cobblestones covering the floor to create a warm, rustic décor. The stones were actually ballast tossed shoreside from anchored ships in the Charleston harbor, but the restaurant's other stone floors were rescued from dismantled slave quarters in Johnston County.

Surrounding one of the main dining rooms is a balcony replicating a loft, complete with hay, pitchforks, and antique farm tools. To complete the homespun atmosphere, the waitresses are costumed in red-checked dresses and white aprons and the waiters in red-checked shirts, blue denim jeans, and white aprons.

The bar features a marble counter top from one of the area's stately old hotels. Its base is constructed from beautiful solid oak doors that once served as the entrance to the hotel's bedrooms. Ah, if only those doors could talk, what stories would be heard!

During the Christmas holidays, a whiff of nostalgia is bound to stir anyone who sees the Barn's gigantic Christmas trees trimmed in the style of the early part of the century, but of course the architecture and the food make dining a meaningful experience at any time.

The restaurant's nostril-tingling Barbecued Spareribs amply fulfill their aromatic promise. The Shrimp Cocktail is a surprise: the shrimp, from the coast of Spain, are so large that they are often mistaken for baby lobsters. Of course, the Barn is famed for its beef, and no one could be disappointed in the variety or quality of the Barn's steaks. They overload the star category with a selection including Chateaubriand, Filet Mignon, beef kabobs, and beef and lobster combinations. In the seafood department, the Barn not only does very special preparations with shrimp scampi, scallops, and flounder for their regular patrons, but they also work with Duke Medical Center's rice diet patients, adhering to the diet's strict requirements for food preparations.

Under owner Thad Eure Jr., the Barn also has a refreshing philosophy which stipulates that the best wine to buy is the wine that suits you best. The beer and wine selection accommodates modestly priced wines as well as a 1959 Château Lafite-Rothschild. The Barn's dessert tray features a broad variety of freshly baked pies, but a pleasant, light delicacy after a scrumptious entrée is the Raspberry Grand Marnier, a sherbet parfait.

Before departing this tasty dose of Americana at its best, stop at the country store, where an antique refrigerator offers many of the Barn's specialties, including the famous Barbecue Sauce.

The Angus Barn is located on U.S. 70 west at Airport Road in Raleigh. Dinner is served from 5:00 to 11:00 p.m. Monday through Saturday, and from 5:00 to 10:00 p.m. on Sundays. The Wild Turkey Lounge opens at 4:00 p.m. The telephone number is (919) 787-3505, and the reservation line is (919) 781-2444.

THE ANGUS BARN'S RASPBERRY GRAND MARNIER

1 quart raspberry sherbet	16 strawberries
1/2 cup raspberry preserves	2 ounces Grand Marnier
1/2 cup white wine	grated peel of 1/2 orange

Combine raspberry preserves with white wine, blending well. Spoon two scoops of raspberry sherbet into each of 4 parfait glasses. Pour wine and preserves over sherbet. Place 4 strawberries in each glass and pour 1/2 ounce Grand Marnier over strawberries. Add a sprinkle of orange peel and serve. Serves 4.

THE ANGUS BARN'S STUFFED POTATOES

6 large Idaho potatoes
½ cup butter
3½ tablespoons grated
  Parmesan cheese
2 tablespoons finely
  crumbled cooked bacon
1 tablespoon sour cream

1 tablespoon chopped
  chives
1 teaspoon salt
½ teaspoon black pepper
⅛ teaspoon monosodium
  glutamate
paprika

Grease potatoes and bake at 400 degrees for 45 minutes. Cut in half lengthwise. Spoon out centers while hot and put in mixing bowl. Save the skins.

Combine all remaining ingredients except paprika, then add to spooned-out potato. Mix with electric mixer for 3 minutes at medium speed. Place mixture in potato skins. Sprinkle lightly with paprika. Brown in hot oven approximately 4 minutes. Serves 8 to 12.

THE ANGUS BARN'S CHOCOLATE CHESS PIE

⅔ cup butter
1⅓ squares unsweetened
  chocolate
1⅓ cups sugar

3 small eggs
⅓ teaspoon salt
1 teaspoon vanilla
1 9-inch piecrust, unbaked

Melt butter and chocolate over boiling water. Mix sugar, eggs, salt, and vanilla; add to chocolate mixture. Pour into pie shell and bake at 375 degrees for about 35 minutes.

CLAIRE'S CAFE AND BAR
Durham

CLAIRE'S CAFE AND BAR

President Lincoln said, "A house divided against itself cannot stand," but the unmarried Mangum sisters didn't believe it. The eccentric Inez and Bessie Mangum divided the home their father had left them with an imaginary line down the center. Due to personality conflicts, each sister lived in only one side of the house. It is said that neighborhood children feared the sisters, who threw rocks at them during those times when one sister locked the other outside.

I thought about the feuding sisters as I passed between the neoclassical porch columns and through the mahogany door of the home, which is under active consideration for the National Register of Historic Places. Leaded glass transoms and interior columns make an impressive statement, which is, no doubt, what Bartlett Mangum had in mind when he built his Colonial Revival home in 1908. At that time the home was directly across from his sawmill, brickyard, and cotton gin.

The bar, with its attractive tile fireplace, was once the home's parlor. I sat at a table beside a window with lace curtains. Crayons are at every table for those who like to doodle while having a drink. My glass of white wine went very well with the two appetizers I sampled, Oysters Imperial and Escargot. The rather mild caviar topping the oysters was softened with Parmesan cheese. Most escargots are done in garlic butter, but at Claire's they use a wonderful mustard sauce.

The biggest surprise was their Lamb Zinfandel. This is a dish for those who don't like lamb, because one taste of this delicious recipe is sure to effect a change of attitude. It reminded me of a great London Broil.

I was anxious to see the rest of this beautifully restored home, so I went upstairs. The yellow heart-pine floor, carpeted in most areas to deter noise, was just one of the bonuses from Mangum's sawmill. As in most homes of this vintage, interesting eccentricities abound. The stair railing, formerly only two and a half feet high, has been raised for safety's sake. One of the upstairs dining rooms is almost entirely round, save for a closet made for someone four feet tall that is now used for liquor storage. Each of the rooms has a fireplace made of a different colored tile, except for one of hand-carved burl made from a single piece of wood.

Downstairs again, I chose their marvelous Buttermilk Pecan Pie, which differs from a conventional pecan pie in its custardlike consistency and its homemade lemon piecrust.

Claire's provides the kind of mellow experience that you could easily take once a week.

Claire's Cafe and Bar is located at 2701 Chapel Hill Road in Durham. Dinner is served from 5:00 until 10:00 p.m. from Sunday through Thursday and from 5:00 until 10:30 p.m. on Friday and Saturday. For reservations call (919) 493-5721.

CLAIRE'S LAMB ZINFANDEL

Marinade:

1/2 cup olive oil	2 teaspoons rosemary
1 cup peanut oil	1 teaspoon dry mustard
1 cup fresh parsley	1 teaspoon mace
1 1/2 tablespoons chopped garlic	1 teaspoon oregano
	1/2 cup sesame oil
1 1/2 tablespoons thyme (whole leaves, if possible)	1 cup soy sauce
	1/2 leg of lamb, boned.

Put olive oil and peanut oil in food processor with parsley, garlic, thyme, rosemary, mustard, mace, and oregano. Blend. Transfer to large bowl and add sesame oil and soy sauce. Cut lamb into steak-size pieces and add to mixture. Cover and marinate for 24 hours to 2 days.

Zinfandel sauce:

3/4 cup strained marinade	1 1/2 cups zinfandel wine (red)

Combine marinade and wine and simmer for about 10 minutes. Take meat out of marinade. Grill on an open flame to desired doneness. While grilling meat, brush on zinfandel sauce. Slice meat at an angle. Top each portion with sauce. Serves 10 to 12.

CLAIRE'S BUTTERMILK PECAN PIE

Lemon crust:

1¼ cups unbleached all-purpose flour	3 tablespoons butter, chilled
¾ tablespoon sugar	1 egg yolk
½ teaspoon salt	1 tablespoon lemon juice
¼ cup shortening, chilled	1 tablespoon ice water

Sift flour, sugar and salt together in a large bowl. Working quickly, rub the shortening and butter into the mixture with fingers or cut with a pastry blender until mixture resembles coarse meal. In a small bowl, mix egg yolk, lemon juice and ice water and drip mixture slowing over the flour mixture while tossing with a fork. Turn the dough out on a large surface and push dough away from you, small bits at a time, with the heel of your hand. Gather dough into a ball and flatten into a circle. Wrap and refrigerate for 2 hours. Roll the dough out to ¼-inch thickness, using as little extra flour as possible. Place in a deep 9-inch pie pan and crimp the edges.

Filling:

½ cup softened butter	3 eggs
4 cups sugar	1 cup buttermilk
3 tablespoons flour	¾ teaspoon vanilla
¼ teaspoon salt	1 cup pecans

Cream butter and sugar in a mixing bowl. Add flour and salt. Add eggs one at a time while beating. Add buttermilk and vanilla and mix until smooth. Sprinkle pecans in bottom of piecrust. Pour in custard. Bake at 375 degrees for 5 minutes; reduce heat to 325 degrees and bake for 1 hour and 25 minutes. Watch edges of piecrust; place aluminum foil over edges to prevent burning if necessary, or lower oven to 300 degrees. Serve warm or cool. Serve with whipped cream or vanilla ice cream if desired. Yields 1 pie.

COLONIAL INN
Hillsborough

COLONIAL INN

When I step from the veranda onto the two-hundred-year-old wide planked floors of the Colonial Inn, I am proud of the quick thinking of our foremother, Sarah Stroud. Besieged by General Sherman's bummers, who were ransacking her inn, that valiant widow lady ran upstairs and waved her husband's Masonic apron from the balcony. Luckily the flag's symbol captured the eye of a sergeant who was a Mason. He ordered his soldiers to return their lootings to the inn.

Say what you will, I believe that symbol, which stood for finer values, stirred the sergeant to uphold a tradition. Who knows, had he not intervened, this venerable old inn might have ended in ashes. Perhaps Sarah could have rebuilt the inn, as it had been rebuilt in 1768 when the original tavern was destroyed by fire, but that is a thought I am glad needs no pondering.

The Colonial Inn continues today to stand for those same traditions of finer values that Mrs. Stroud was determined to preserve. I speak not only of the craftsmanship that was born from the ethic of building structures to last; I include the cooks' expertise in preparing the aristocracy of Southern cooking.

Amidst the friendliness that adds something special to the intimate dining rooms, you may enjoy Fried Chicken, Country Ham, or fresh seafood. This Southern-style cooking that is not overcooked, oversalted, or overgreasy, as unfortunately is often the case.

However, the Colonial Inn's owners, Carolyn Welsh and Evelyn Atkins, told me honestly that the fare is not for dieters, and for the most part they are correct. My calorie count tilted when I ate everything on a plate filled with Country Ham, Potatoes, Hot Biscuits, and Red Eye Gravy, all of which I embellished with half a bottle of Beaujolais. However, you could—yes, you could—diet with the Broiled Fresh Flounder or Ribeye Steak and a tossed salad. You would have to pass up the Apple Cobbler or Black Walnut Pie, as I did, but my feeling is that you need not pass up the Colonial Inn because you're trying to trim.

The Colonial Inn is located at 153 West King Street in Hillsborough. Lunch is served from 11:30 a.m. to 2:00 p.m. and dinner from 5:00 to 9:00 p.m., Tuesday through Saturday. On Sunday, family-style serving is from 11:30 a.m. to 8:00 p.m. For reservations call (919) 732-2461.

COLONIAL INN'S CORNWALLIS YAMS

6 medium sweet potatoes
1½ cups milk
1 cup sugar
½ cup crushed pineapple
½ cup butter
3 eggs, beaten

½ teaspoon salt
½ teaspoon ground
  cinnamon
½ teaspoon ground nutmeg
½ cup flaked coconut

Wash sweet potatoes and place in a large saucepan; cover with water and bring to a boil. Cover pan and simmer about 30 minutes. Peel and mash the potatoes. Add all remaining ingredients except coconut and mix well. Pour into a greased 13- by 9- by 2-inch baking dish. Bake at 350 degrees for 45 minutes. Sprinkle with coconut. Serves 12 to 14.

COLONIAL INN'S BAKED APPLES

6 large baking apples
6 tablespoons sugar
1½ teaspoons ground
  cinnamon
1½ teaspoons ground
  nutmeg

2 tablespoons butter
½ to ¾ cup apple juice
red food coloring (optional)

Peel and core apples and place in a shallow 2-quart casserole. Pour 1 tablespoon sugar into the hole of each apple. Sprinkle each with cinnamon and nutmeg and top with 1 teaspoon butter. Heat apple juice to boiling and add red food coloring; pour juice into casserole. Bake uncovered at 400 degrees for 50 to 60 minutes, or until tender. Brush occasionally with juice. Serves 6.

COLONIAL INN'S
GREEN BEANS AMANDINE

2 pounds fresh green beans   ⅓ cup minced onion
1 small ham hock   ⅔ cup sliced almonds
3 tablespoons butter   1 tablespoon salt

Remove strings from green beans. Cut beans into 1½-inch pieces and wash thoroughly. Place in a 5-quart Dutch oven and add the ham hock and water to cover. Bring to a boil and reduce heat. Cover and simmer for 1 hour. Drain off excess liquid. Sauté onions and almonds in butter until onions are transparent. Add beans and salt. Toss lightly. Serves 8.

THE FEARRINGTON HOUSE
Chapel Hill

THE FEARRINGTON HOUSE

After traveling south for about eight miles on U.S. 15—501 from Chapel Hill, you'll look to your left and feel as if you'd stumbled upon a Southern Grandma Moses painting. An old dairy barn and silo sit beyond a lush green meadow. This is one of the soothing views available to the guests of The Fearrington House, a restaurant in a traditional white Colonial home.

When my friend and I visited the restaurant for Sunday brunch, we sat on a brick-floored back porch. We had two appealing views: one of the restaurant's herb garden, the harvest of which is used in the food preparations, and another of a large rose garden. The rose garden presents the perfect backdrop for the white latticework patio used during warm weather.

No detail has been spared by Fearrington's owner and decorator, Jenny Fitch. Her deft hand has made each of the seven dining rooms of the restaurant into a tasteful blend of color and comfort. I adored the relaxed country feel of chintz and cotton print lounges sitting behind the wooden tables. Each table was covered with matching laminated prints and was accented with homegrown flowers. The flowers were displayed in such imaginative containers as bird cages and vases covered in broom straw, which lent a piquant charm to the pastoral setting.

A pleasing atmosphere always adds an extra measure to my meal. My brunch was no exception. It featured a dish of cold shrimp, scallops, and vegetables that was as pretty to look at as it was appetizing. A perfect for dieting, if you can refrain from dipping into the Mayonnaise Sauce. My friend enjoyed the Vegetarian Ratatouille plate. Best of all is the Bourbon Pecan Pie, but my friend said that her Lemon Chess Pie was a close second.

The most popular entrée for evening dining is Veal in Madeira Sauce with Asparagus, or Roast Duck with Lingonberry Sauce. Special diets can be accommodated if the restaurant is given twenty-four hours' notice. The Fearrington House offers a wonderful selection of California wines.

After brunch we enjoyed walking through the grape arbor

at the rear of the house and visiting the studio of Jim Pringle, a potter. A fourteen-room country inn was added to the Fearrington House in 1986. The Fitches plan to recycle the old dairy barn by making it a country market. There shoppers will find flowers, vegetables, and the wares of the craftsmen who are converting the old silo and other outbuildings on the Fearrington estate into working studios. This conversion will give even sharper punctuation to the Grandma Moses landscape.

The Fearrington House is eight miles south of Chapel Hill on U.S. 15—501. Dinner is served from 6:00 to 9:00 p.m. Tuesday through Saturday, and Sunday dinner is served from 4:30 to 7:00 p.m. For reservations call (919) 542-2121.

THE FEARRINGTON HOUSE'S
ROAST PORK LOIN

1 whole pork loin	2 tablespoons rosemary
1 cup brown sugar	1 tablespoon garlic powder
1 cup Plochmann's mustard	2 teaspoons salt
2 tablespoons sage	1/2 teaspoon pepper

Split and debone pork loin. Blend other ingredients together and rub half over inside of pork. Tie meat securely with string. Rub remaining mixture over outside of pork. Roast at 350 degrees until an internal temperature of 155 degrees is reached.
Serve with mustard butter (see recipe below). Serves 4 to 6.

THE FEARRINGTON HOUSE'S
MUSTARD BUTTER

1/2 cup butter, softened	4 tablespoons Plochmann's
1/2 clove garlic, pressed	mustard
juice of 1/2 lemon	

Whip butter until soft. Whip in remaining ingredients.

THE FEARRINGTON HOUSE'S
BOURBON PECAN PIE

Pastry:

1 cup plus 2 tablespoon all-
purpose flour
pinch of salt
¼ cup butter

2 tablespoons vegetable
shortening
¼ cup cold water

Add the shortening and butter to the flour and salt, and work the mixture with fingertips until it resembles corn-flakes. Blend in the water until all the ingredients can be worked into a ball. Chill. Roll out dough and fit into a 9-inch pie pan. Fill with pie weights or dry beans to keep the sides from collapsing, and bake at 425 degrees for 5 minutes. Remove from oven and lower temperature to 350 degrees.

Filling:

3 eggs
½ teaspoon salt
1 cup light Karo syrup

1 cup sugar
1 tablespoon bourbon
1 cup chopped pecan pieces

Mix all ingredients and pour into the shell. Bake for 45 to 60 minutes or until the pie is firm to the touch. Serve with freshly whipped cream or homemade vanilla ice cream. Serves 6.

RESTAURANT LA RESIDENCE
Chapel Hill

RESTAURANT LA RESIDENCE

I'd venture to say few people know that the favorite dish of Dean Smith is veal kidneys. The management of La Résidence knows; each time the famed basketball coach of the University of North Carolina makes a reservation, the supply of kidneys is checked so that there will be no disappointment to the frequent guest. I imagine that even without the kidneys most diners would be hard pressed to find a source of disappointment in the restaurant's continental cuisine prepared with the classic French techniques.

French cooking seems at first a bit incongruous in a building constructed in 1926 as a Baptist rectory, but the interior has been stylishly decorated in a country French motif. Each dining room presents a unique personality, ranging from a casual look with black-eyed Susans in an earthenware pitcher set upon a primitive antique sideboard, to a more sophisticated room dressed in a rich verdant color scheme. This room's fabric-covered banquettes are supplied with comfortably squashy pillows that present an invitation to lounge about as you might picture yourself in a chic Parisian salon. The restaurant now operates the outdoor Cafe Perdu, which serves from a casual menu from April through October.

The main restaurant serves a continually evolving repertoire of enticing dishes. The nouvelle cuisine is lighter than the usual French fare, but if you are truly trying to de-escalate your calorie intake, the chefs will be happy to poach or broil a number of special dishes with wine and herbs.

The wine list offers a carefully chosen selection of both imported and domestic vintages, plus a small but adequate selection of imported beers. A bar has recently been added.

When I asked about the restaurant's marvelous Espresso Ice Cream, I was told that the base recipe came originally from *Food & Wine* magazine but had gradually evolved into an entirely new taste. You can imagine the chef's surprise when *Food & Wine* passed along a reader's request for the recipe for La Résidence's ice cream. Naturally, the restaurant was only too pleased to share its success, which may be part of the reason La Résidence has been highly acclaimed by not only *Food & Wine*, but *Fortune* and *Holiday* magazines. The restaurant has won the Travel-Holiday Award every year since 1981. You may be sure that it is an award winner in my travels

Restaurant La Résidence is located at 220 West Rosemary Street in Chapel Hill. Dinner is served from 6:00 until 9:00 p.m. Sunday through Thursday and from 6:00 until 9:30 p.m. on Friday and Saturday. For reservations call (919) 967-2506.

LA RESIDENCE'S COLD BLUEBERRY SOUP

2 pints fresh blueberries
¼ bottle Beaujolais
1 10-ounce bottle apricot
  nectar
grated peel of 2 lemons

½ tablespoon coarse black
  pepper
pinch of salt
1 cup sour cream
¼ pint sliced strawberries

Put blueberries through a sieve or food mill. Add Beaujolais, apricot nectar, lemon peel and salt and pepper. Stir and chill. Garnish each bowl of soup with a generous dollop of sour cream and sliced strawberries. Serves 6.

LA RESIDENCE'S FILET MIGNON
WITH SAUCE RAIFORT

6 to 8 beef fillets
1 pound unsalted butter
½ cup fresh chives, minced
5 tablespoons prepared
  horseradish

3 tablespoons lemon juice
4 cloves garlic, pressed

With electric mixer cream butter and mix in chives, horseradish, lemon juice and garlic. Blend well. Cover bowl and refrigerate until firm. Broil meat slightly on both sides; place a generous dollop of butter on each fillet and broil until butter melts. Use leftover sauce for other grilled meats and fresh vegetables. Serves 8.

LA RESIDENCE'S PORK WITH MUSTARD SAUCE

6 half-inch boned pork loin
  chops
1/4 cup or more Wondra
  flour
1 tablespoon dry mustard
3 tablespoons butter
3 tablespoons lemon juice

4 tablespoons brandy
1/3 cup Pommery mustard
1 cup heavy cream
salt and pepper to taste
6 cornichon pickles
1/2 pound cooked fettucine

Lightly coat the pork with a mixture of the flour and dry mustard. Sauté the pork in butter over a medium to high heat until light brown on each side. Add the prepared mustard, cream and salt and pepper. Stir the sauce until it is hot, then add the pork and cook slowly over a low heat until thoroughly cooked. Serve with hot fettucine and garnish with cornichons. Serves 6.

LA RESIDENCE'S ESPRESSO ICE CREAM

1 3/4 cups half-and-half
2 tablespoons instant coffee
9 egg yolks
1/8 teaspoon salt
3/4 cup sugar
1 1/2 cups whipping cream

6 tablespoons unsalted
  butter
1 tablespoon vanilla
1/4 cup ground espresso
  coffee

Mix half-and-half with instant coffee and scald in small saucepan. Beat egg yolks with salt in large bowl, gradually adding sugar until mixture is light and fluffy. Slowly add half- and-half, beating constantly. Transfer to heavy saucepan and cook over medium heat, stirring, until mixture thickens. Do not let mixture boil. Blend in cream and butter, and let cool.

Stir in vanilla. Strain. Pour into ice cream freezer and churn until desired consistency. Fold in espresso. Allow to set up in freezer at least 30 minutes before serving. Yields 2 quarts.

FRAN'S FRONT PORCH
Liberty

FRAN'S FRONT PORCH

Could business be so good that it threatens to put you out of business? That's exactly what happened when Fran Holt and daughters Carolyn Beyer and Sylvia Belvin opened Fran's Front Porch in the 1911 home of Fran's birth. The restaurant opened on a Wednesday, because the local newspaper came out that day. The food critic's review so inundated the restaurant with guests that Fran, Carolyn, and Sylvia ran out of food. The whole family was recruited to meet the crisis. Sons-in-law, uncles, and aunts spent the whole night cooking and bringing in fresh supplies. Still, they could not meet the demand that first week.

As Carolyn recalled, "Some people start business on a shoestring, but we started with a yard sale." They bought two sixty-five-dollar stoves and a refrigerator with the proceeds, which put the lovely old farmhouse with its wraparound porch into business. Only a small loan was available, as bankers didn't feel that people would travel to the country to eat. The restaurant opened in 1976, and now there is a small private airport across the road. People actually fly in and walk a quarter of a mile just to eat Fran's wonderful Southern cooking.

My daughter Heather and I arrived late on a warm summer evening. An abundance of ferns and blooming flowers decorates the entire porch, making it a lovely place to dine. Inside, there is a buffet-style arrangement. Being selective isn't easy because you'll want to try everything. We began with green beans, cabbage, red beans, squash casserole, cooked apples, the best chicken pie I've ever tasted, juicy roast beef, perfectly baked green peppers, and hot rolls. Another table was laden with salads. Vegetarians love to dine here because the vegetables are seasoned with vegetable oil, though I'd almost swear I tasted the traditional ham flavor.

Fran's is known for its desserts, especially the tangy, sweet Lemon Chess Pie, which I would fly in for any day. Heather leaned toward their wonderful Chocolate Cream Pie and Peter Paul Mounds Cake. I feel that Fran and her daughters' culinary efforts are the epitome of true Southern cooking. This is definitely a restaurant to visit when you are starved.

Fran's Front Porch is located at 6139 Smithwood Road in Liberty. Dinner is served from 5:00 until 8:30 p.m. Thursday through Saturday. Sunday lunch is served from noon until 2:30 p.m. The telephone number is (919) 685-4104.

FRAN'S LEMON CHESS PIE

2 cups sugar
1 tablespoon cornmeal
1 tablespoon plain flour
4 eggs
1/4 cup melted butter
1/4 cup milk

4 tablespoons lemon rind, grated
1/4 cup lemon juice
1 9-inch pie shell or 2 smaller pie shells

Put sugar, cornmeal and flour in a bowl; toss lightly with fork. Add eggs, butter, milk, lemon rind and lemon juice. Beat with mixer until smooth. Pour into 1 9-inch pie shell or 2 smaller pie shells. Bake at 375 degrees for 35 to 45 minutes until firm. Yields 1 or 2 pies.

FRAN'S CHICKEN PIE

Crust:
1/2 cup water
1 cup pure lard
3 cups plain flour

1/2 teaspoon salt
1/2 teaspoon baking powder

Boil water and add lard, stirring until melted. Remove from heat. Add flour, salt, and baking powder, mixing well. Roll into ball, cover and chill.

Filling:
4- to 5-pound chicken
1/2 cup margarine
1 1/2 cups milk

5 tablespoons cornstarch
1/4 cup cold water
salt and pepper to taste

Cook chicken in lightly salted water. When tender, re-

71

move chicken, reserving broth. Remove chicken from bones and cut into small pieces. Strain chicken broth and measure 3 cups into a 3-quart pot. Add margarine and milk, bringing to a boil. Dissolve cornstarch in ¼ cup cold water and add to the broth mixture, stirring constantly until a gravy is obtained. Add chicken, salt and pepper. Pour mixture into a 9- by 13- by 2-inch greased pan. Roll out crust and cover top. Bake at 400 to 425 degrees for 40 to 45 minutes until brown. Yields 1 pie.

THE POLLIROSA
Tobaccoville

THE POLLIROSA

Back when The Pollirosa restaurant's two-story log structure was used as a residence, a community Dutch oven was attached to one side of it. Women of the area would gather there and bake up to fifty pies at a time, and as the women cooked, the men would fiddle.

The Hauser family brought the Moravian tradition of "making music when breaking bread" from Germany when they immigrated to Pennsylvania in 1757. Eight generations later, Millie and Johnny Rierson revived that tradition when, in 1965, they opened The Pollirosa, a restaurant that serves old-fashioned food and old-time music.

The restaurant is named for two of the family's best cooks: Polly Shamel, who lived in the log plantation house during the Civil War, and Rosa Rierson, who became its resident during the days of the community oven. The tradition of their cooking lives on in The Pollirosa's menu, which features such dishes as Chicken and Dumplings, fresh home-grown vegetables, and the best Pound Cake you've ever put in your mouth.

The popularity of The Pollirosa is proven by the fact that when the main structure burned a few years ago, the loyal clientele helped with the fund raising necessary to rebuild. The main dining room was rebuilt, and a large music hall was added. Gospel groups and the Rierson family's country-and-western band provide the entertainment.

Music and food are equally pleasurable, and both are offered for one incredibly low price. You can even get a return trip for seconds. When I asked Mrs. Rierson how she and her husband could offer so much for so little, she just smiled and said, "Cooperation—between us, the good Lord, and the good earth."

The Pollirosa is located on Hollyberry Lane off Spainhour Mill Road in Tobaccoville, which is 15 miles north of Winston-Salem on U.S. 52. Dinner is served from 4:30 to 8:30 p.m. on Friday and Saturday. For reservations call (919) 983-5352.

THE POLLIROSA'S CUCUMBER PICKLES

1 quart vinegar
2 quarts water
3 gallons cucumbers

1 teaspoon canning salt per
jar
6 teaspoons sugar per jar

In large pot, place water and vinegar. Bring to a boil and add fresh, clean cucumbers, whole or sliced. Cucumbers should remain only long enough to change to an olive green color, but should not boil. Pack cucumbers in sterilized glass quart jars and add one teaspoon salt and six teaspoons sugar to each jar. Fill each jar with vinegar and water to ½ inch from top. Seal jars. Yields about 12 quarts.

THE POLLIROSA'S GRAHAM CRACKER CAKE

1 cup butter
2 cups sugar
5 eggs
2 teaspoons baking powder
1 pound graham crackers,
  crushed

1 cup milk
1 cup flaked coconut
1 large can pineapple,
  drained

Cream butter and sugar; add eggs, one at a time, and mix well. In a separate bowl, add baking powder to graham cracker crumbs. Stir into moist ingredients. Add milk and coconut, mixing well. Pour into 3 greased and floured cake pans. Bake at 350 degrees for 25 to 30 minutes. Remove from oven and cool. Place one layer of cake on a plate spread with ⅓ of crushed pineapple; repeat procedure with remaining layers and add icing (see recipe below).

THE POLLIROSA'S ICING
FOR GRAHAM CRACKER CAKE

½ cup butter
1 egg

1 box confectioners sugar
1 teaspoon vanilla

Soften butter, beat egg and mix at low speed. Add vanilla and fold in confectioners sugar. Ice cooled cake.

THE POLLIROSA'S BEST POUND CAKE

3 cups sugar
½ cup margarine
1 cup shortening
6 eggs
½ teaspoon vanilla extract

½ teaspoon lemon extract
pinch of salt
3½ cups sifted plain or
cake flour

Cream sugar, margarine and shortening. Beat eggs and add to mixture; add vanilla, lemon and salt. Slowly add flour, mixing thoroughly. Pour batter in a greased bundt or pound cake pan. Bake at 300 degrees for 45 minutes, then raise the temperature to 325 degrees and bake for another 45 minutes.

OLD SALEM TAVERN
Winston-Salem

OLD SALEM TAVERN

No, George Washington never ate here. He did, however, sleep next door at the original Salem Tavern for two nights in 1791. I would imagine that he bypassed the "publick room" where the "ordinary" were served, and ate instead in the "gentlemen's room," which was located directly across the hall. Can't you just visualize one of your ancestors smoking a long clay pipe and rubbing shoulders—or more probably, lifting a tankard of ale—with the Father of Our Country?

Today, as you sit in a Windsor chair at a table set with pewter plates, the Tavern's waiters and waitresses in period costumes are certain to treat you with the same "kindness and cordiality" that was stipulated by the original Moravian elders. The Moravians, a devout Germanic people, immigrated to Pennsylvania to escape religious persecution in the 1730s. A segment of these methodical people migrated to North Carolina in 1753 and eventually built a planned community, keeping intact their strict code of morality. Records note that the brethren didn't frown on the use of spirits; it was the "deleterious influence of strangers" that caused them to limit the tavern, when they could, to "traveling strangers only." By the time of the Revolution, the tavern was famous throughout the Southeast for the high quality of its "entertainment," a term meaning, as it does today, "good food and drink taken amid hospitable surroundings." The tavern became so popular that by 1815 it was necessary to build the current tavern to house the overflow. It is in this tavern that you may dine beside a traditional Moravian fireplace or under a candle in a sconce that makes a flickering butterfly-shaped shadow against the foot-thick walls.

In the warmer months, my preference is the wisteria-cloaked arbor, where I always enjoy the Moravian Chicken Pie or Cornmeal Mush with Tomato Sauce.

At dinner I am inclined toward Rack of Lamb dusted with rosemary and bread crumbs or Deviled Duck. For dessert I can never pass up their unbelievably rich Chocolate Amaretto Pie. You may be refreshed by a wide selection of "spirits" that remain part of the Tavern's hospitality.

When you visit Old Salem Tavern, set aside a day for seeing the restored village of Old Salem. You'll realize that Salem, whose name was taken from the Hebrew word meaning peace, continues to impart the same serene atmosphere as it did in yestertime.

Old Salem Tavern is located at 736 South Main Street in Winston-Salem. Lunch is served from 11:30 a.m. until 2:00 p.m. Sunday through Friday and from 11:30 a.m. until 2:30 p.m. on Saturday. Dinner is served from 5:30 until 9:00 p.m. Monday through Thursday and from 5:30 until 9:30 p.m. on Friday and Saturday. For reservations call (919) 748-8585.

OLD SALEM TAVERN'S
CHOCOLATE AMARETTO PIE

Crust:

1½ cups chocolate cookies, crumbled	¼ cup melted butter
½ cup almond paste, crumbled	

Put cookies into a food processor and process until they are the consistency of crumbs. Add almond paste and butter and process until blended. Spread evenly into a 9½- or 10-inch, deep pie pan. Bake in a preheated 400-degree oven for 5 minutes. Remove and cool.

Filling:

1 egg yolk	2 tablespoons rum
2 tablespoons almond paste	16 ounces semisweet
2 tablespoons instant coffee	chocolate
1 cup whipping cream	¼ cup melted butter
1 tablespoon brandy	2 egg whites
2 tablespoons amaretto liqueur	2 tablespoons powdered sugar

In food processor, add egg yolk, almond paste, coffee, 3 tablespoons of the whipping cream, brandy, amaretto and rum. Process until smooth. In double boiler, melt chocolate over hot (not boiling) water. Add melted chocolate and butter to the mixture and process until blended. Let cool. In an electric mixer, beat egg whites with powdered sugar. Beat in remaining whipping cream. Fold into chocolate mixture gently. Pour into piecrust. Refrigerate 4 hours. Yields 1 pie.

OLD SALEM TAVERN'S CORNMEAL MUSH

6 strips bacon, diced
3/4 cup chopped onion
2 cups water
1 cup coarsely ground
  cornmeal
salt and pepper to taste
3/4 cup ham, cubed
3/4 cup white cheddar
  cheese, shredded

flour
1 egg, beaten
1/2 cup bread crumbs
2 tablespoons vegetable oil
Tomato Sauce (recipe
  follows)

In a heavy skillet, fry the bacon with the onion. Add water and bring to a boil. Stir in the cornmeal and cook over low heat until thick and smooth. Add salt and pepper, ham and cheese. Pour into a flat pan and chill until set. Cut into diamonds and coat with flour, then with egg, then with bread crumbs. Fry in oil and serve with Tomato Sauce. Serves 6.

OLD SALEM TAVERN'S TOMATO SAUCE

2 tablespoons bacon fat
2 tablespoons olive oil
1 medium onion, finely
  chopped
1 clove garlic, chopped
1 stalk celery, chopped

3 cups tomatoes, peeled
  and diced
salt and pepper to taste
1 teaspoon sugar
2 to 3 tablespoons red wine

Place bacon fat and olive oil in saucepan and fry onion, garlic and celery until soft. Add tomatoes and simmer for 15 to 20 minutes. Season with salt and pepper, sugar and red wine. Serves 8 or more.

ZEVELY HOUSE
Winston-Salem

ZEVELY HOUSE

You get the feeling that Van Nieman Zevely, the cabinet-maker who built Zevely House in 1815, and its current owners and chefs, Ken Martin and Thomas "Alex" Alexander, were cut from the same cloth. It seems that Zevely defied Moravian custom by refusing to ask the church elders for permission to marry his fiancée, Johanna Shober. Later this faux pas was corrected, but not, one would imagine, soon enough to satisfy the ostracized Miss Shober. Therefore, the owners say chuckling, "When the other restaurant was built next door, it seemed only right to call it Johanna Shober's."

As you listen to Martin and Alexander describe the agony and frustration when the wonderful old Flemish brick house was moved to the downtown's fashionable West End, where it stands as the oldest structure in Winston township, you recognize their special feelings for sturdy architecture. "It had to be saved," they said. And saved it was, through months of meticulous restoration.

Now you may dine in a blue and white, antique-filled setting. Zevely was not a pretentious man, nor are Ken and Alex, who prefer to preserve a casual atmosphere with a menu as unintimidating in price as it is in choice. You can order anything from a good hamburger, with an accent on good, to Veal Cordon Bleu.

For lunch I like the Seafood au Gratin followed by a bowl of French Onion Soup, and all topped off with the famous Pumpkin Muffins. The muffins have become such a trademark that Ken and Alex had one enshrined in plastic at the bar.

At dinner I rack my brain trying to choose, because it's all fantastic! The Beef Filet with Sauce Van Nieman is "wunderbar," but so is the Stir-fry Chicken. Dieters can feast on a Lemon-broiled Carolina Mountain Rainbow Trout. If I'm allowed a dessert I'll choose the super Turtle Pie.

You'll discover an enticing selection of mixed drinks, or you may choose one of the beers or one of the thirty excellent California and French wines to complement your meal.

Zevely House is located at 901 West Fourth Street in Winston-Salem. Lunch is served from 11:30 a.m. until 1:30 p.m. Monday through Friday. Dinner is served from 5:30 until 9:00 p.m. Monday through Saturday. Sunday brunch is served from 11:30 a.m. until 1:30 p.m. For reservations call (919) 725-6666.

ZEVELY HOUSE'S BEEF FILETS VAN NIEMAN

salt and pepper to taste
4 8-ounce beef filets, cut
   from tenderloin
6 tablespoons cream cheese,
   softened
1/2 cup sour cream

1 cup whipping cream
1 tablespoon brandy
3/4 cup chutney, strained
1 tablespoon sesame seeds,
   toasted

Salt and pepper filets and grill them to desired doneness. In a saucepan, place cream cheese, sour cream, whipping cream and brandy and mix over low heat; reduce slightly and stir in chutney. Cook until mixture reaches desired consistency. Spoon sauce over meat and garnish with sesame seeds. Serves 4.

ZEVELY HOUSE'S PUMPKIN MUFFINS

1 cup or more canned
   pumpkin
2 eggs
1/3 cup water
1/3 cup butter, melted
12/3 cups sifted flour
11/2 cups sugar
1/3 cup raisins

1 teaspoon baking soda
1 teaspoon pumpkin pie
   spice
1/4 teaspoon salt
1/4 teaspoon baking powder
1/8 teaspoon ground cloves
18 paper muffin liners
Pam

Mix wet ingredients thoroughly; add dry ingredients, and stir until blended. Spray paper liners with Pam and fill them 2/3 full. Bake at 350 degrees until golden brown, about 35 minutes. Yields 18.

ZEVELY HOUSE'S FRENCH ONION SOUP

5 medium onions
3 quarts beef stock
2 tablespoons butter

dash of white wine
10 slices Swiss cheese
2 cups croutons

Slice onions thin. Place in a large pot and cover with beef stock. Cook on medium-high for about an hour. Add salt and pepper, wine and butter. Pour into individual oven-proof soup bowls and top with a slice of Swiss cheese and croutons; place under broiler until cheese melts. Serves 10.

ZEVELY HOUSE'S POTATO CAKES
WITH SOUR CREAM AND CAVIARS

2 large baking potatoes
1 to 2 tablespoons clarified
   butter or vegetable oil
4 tablespoons sour cream
2 teaspoons each of red,
   black, and gold caviar

1 tablespoon fresh chives,
   chopped
1 tablespoon chopped
   scallions

Bake potatoes and grate; shape into 4 patties. Place butter or oil in skillet and sauté patties. Place patties on plates and add a tablespoon of sour cream and ½ teaspoon of each caviar to each patty. Garnish with chives or scallions or both. (Do not add salt as there is sufficient seasoning in the caviars.) Serves 4.

LA CHAUDIERE
Winston-Salem

LA CHAUDIERE

True Gallic charm greets you the moment you step upon the terra-cotta tiled floor of La Chaudière. Now, who but the innovative French would think of converting a furnace room into one of North Carolina's most superb restaurants? The original owners converted a group of rooms that heated, through a maze of underground tunnels, the vast R. J. Reynolds estate. In fact, the room that currently is the wine cellar served as the original entrance to the underground passageway, which was built in 1917.

Is there a dungeonlike feeling? No, indeed. The antique windows, French doors, and profusion of red geraniums produce a light and airy country French atmosphere. Even foot-thick plaster walls are amusingly adorned with antique prints, tapestry reproductions, and fine watercolors.

The first time I dined at La Chaudière I ordered the Rack of Lamb Grilled with Herbs, Escargots de Bourgogne, and a salad. Voila! My dinner companions raved about an appetizer of shrimp in puff pastry and Saga cheese, which they claim has addicted them.

The artistic pastry chef can even make the puff pastry encasing crabmeat resemble a baby crab. I discovered why my pastries don't taste like his. He works in a pastry room kept at an even sixty degrees. My two favorite desserts are Boite aux Chocolat, which is rum-soaked cake and butter cream covered in chocolate, and a layered praline meringue called Sucées. It certainly was a success.

The chef recommended the Poulet au Riesling, adding that you must never cook with a wine that you wouldn't serve at your table. For dieters, he suggested the Terrine de Legumes with a vinaigrette sauce, and said they would "decalorize" any dish for you if given sufficient notice.

My appreciation goes to the restaurant's owners, Thad and Catherine Jones, for providing an elegant yet casual approach to dining with the charmingly different French sense of humor.

La Chaudière is located in Reynolda Village at 120 Reynolda Road in Winston-Salem. Dinner is served from 6:00

until 9:30 p.m. Tuesday through Saturday, and 6:00 until 9:00 p.m. on Sundays. For reservations call (919) 748-0269.

LA CHAUDIERE'S
POACHED FISH MARSEILLAISE

Stock:

2 2- to 3-pound whole red snappers*

3 stalks celery, chopped

1 small onion, chopped

2 bay leaves

1/2 teaspoon fresh thyme

Fillet fish and reserve flesh. Place heads and bones in a medium saucepan, cover with water, and heat until barely rolling. Add celery, onion, bay leaves, and thyme and heat for 45 minutes. Strain stock.

*If only fillets are available, 1 8-ounce bottle of clam juice may be used for stock instead of heads and bones.

Red snapper:

2 cups dry white wine

3/4 cup vermouth

1 shallot, chopped

1 head fresh fennel or 1/2 teaspoon fennel seeds

1/4 cup butter

8 strands saffron or 1/2 teaspoon powdered saffron

1 tablespoon flour

1/3 cup heavy whipping cream

1 ounce Pernod

salt and pepper to taste

Divide fish into 4 portions, folding ends under the middle. Place stock and fish in a heavy aluminum or stainless steel skillet slightly larger than the size of the fish. Add wine, vermouth, and shallot. Cover and poach the fish slowly at medium-low for 7 to 9 minutes. Remove fish from pan and place on an ovenproof plate; cover and place in a 150-degree oven or other warm place. Remove core from fennel and discard. Slice fennel fine. Melt 2 tablespoons of the butter in a small saucepan and sauté fennel until it begins to change color. Add 1/2 to 3/4 cup of stock and stir in saffron. Simmer about 5 minutes. Boil remaining stock until volume is reduced by half. Place remaining 2 tablespoons of butter and flour in a small sauté pan and stir over low heat until a smooth paste forms. Whisk into stock until mixture is an even consistency. Whisk in cream, Pernod and fennel mixture until well mixed. Boil, stirring periodically, until sauce binds to spoon. Add salt and pepper. Place fish on warmed plates and ladle stock evenly over fish. Serves 4.

STARS
Winston-Salem

STARS

In the lower lobby of Winston-Salem's art-nouveau Stevens Center theatre complex is a magnificent restaurant named Stars. A few years back I included this restaurant, then under different ownership, in a magazine article. When I learned that it had gone through a rebirth under the nurturing tutelage of famed food impresario Gayle Winston, I couldn't wait to visit. Gayle Winston is one of those rare people who has as much respect for superb cooking as she does for historical preservation. The building is a former 1929 movie palace, and I don't use the word palace lightly. When I was knee-high to a grasshopper and went to the movies, this was the kind of place in fashion—a majestic homage to architecture.

Of all Gayle Winston's restaurants, Stars is unquestionably the most elegant in appearance. Rose-colored walls dramatized by the original gold bas-relief and satin-etched mirrors reach to the second-floor mezzanine of the theatre.

My daughter Heather and I waded through the rich, deep green carpeting to our table to enjoy a range of food that is as refined or as simple as you like—from Red Salmon Caviar with blini and sour cream to Chili. We began with a unique Seviche that is easy to make but tastes like you slaved for hours. I particularly enjoyed their Caesar Salad, which was prepared tableside. Heather voted, bite after bite, for their Grilled Duck Breast with Raspberry and Ginger Sauce, and I for the Lemon Chicken in a heavenly Sweet and Sour Sauce. For my vegetarian friends, I recommend their herbed Crêpes Gateau layered with spinach, mushrooms and carrots.

Do you know why we could still eat dessert? Because you can order either a "grazing," which is a small portion at half the price, or a full entrée. We shared their Triple Chocolate Marjolaine, a combination of light and dark chocolate mousses with praline cream, and a Coffee Almond Torte, which, for the first time in my experience, won out over chocolate. Not that the Marjolaine was one whit less delicious, but the Torte was delicately different. Not unlike Stars—deliciously different. I promise, no one will ever mistake it for the original coffee shop there called Mom's Service.

Stars is located in the Stevens Center at 401 West Fourth Street in Winston-Salem. Meals are presently served in conjunction with Stevens Center productions, special events, and private parties, but plans are to expand the schedule to full-time operation in the near future. For information call (919) 761-0476.

STARS' COFFEE ALMOND TORTE

Cake:

½ cup bread crumbs
4 egg whites (reserve 3 yolks)
½ cup sugar
2 cups blanched almonds, ground (reserve ¼ cup)

3 tablespoons bread crumbs
1½ tablespoons instant coffee granules
4 tablespoons brewed coffee, hot

Butter 2 8-inch cake pans liberally. Divide ½ cup bread crumbs and sprinkle over bottom and sides, shaking to cover evenly. Beat egg whites with electric mixer until stiff. Gently fold in sugar, 1¾ cups almonds, 3 tablespoons bread crumbs and coffee granules a little at a time manually until incorporated. Spread batter into cake pans and bake in a preheated 350-degree oven for 25 minutes. Remove and sprinkle each cake with 2 tablespoons of coffee.

Icing:

1 cup heavy cream
5 tablespoons unsalted butter
1 cup confectioners sugar

3 egg yolks
¼ cup almonds
1 tablespoon instant coffee granules

Whip cream until stiff and refrigerate. Cream butter and sugar in electric mixer until mixture is lemon-colored. Add egg yolks one at a time until smooth. Gently fold almonds, whipped cream and coffee granules into mixture manually. Spread icing thickly over bottom layer of cake. Add top layer and spread icing over top and sides. Refrigerate at least 4 hours. Yields 1 cake.

STARS' SEVICHE

1 pound bay scallops
¼ cup or more fresh lime
  juice
1 tomato, peeled, seeded
  and diced
1 chopped red onion
2 chopped jalapeno peppers

3 to 4 chopped black olives
¼ cup fresh parsley or
  cilantro, minced
salt and fresh-ground
  pepper to taste
¼ cup olive oil

Clean scallops and cover with lime juice in a bowl. Marinate overnight in refrigerator. Drain scallops and combine with all remaining ingredients. Sprinkle with fresh lime juice. Serves 6.

STARS' CAESAR SALAD

3 to 4 drops olive oil
fresh black pepper, ground
  coarse
2 anchovies
2 cloves garlic, chopped
  fine
2 egg yolks
¼ cup olive oil

juice of ½ lemon
¼ teaspoon dry mustard
½ teaspoon ground pepper
1 head romaine lettuce
¼ cup freshly grated
  Parmesan cheese
¼ cup croutons

Season the bottom of a wooden bowl with 3 to 4 drops of oil and a little ground pepper. Add anchovies, crushing with fork until they become a paste. Blend garlic with anchovies. Add egg yolks and whisk until very smooth. Slowly drizzle ¼ cup of oil down sides of bowl while turning bowl slowly. Whisk briskly until mixture thickens. Add lemon juice, mustard and ½ teaspoon ground pepper and whisk until well-blended. Add torn romaine, cheese and croutons. Toss. Serves 2.

TANGLEWOOD MANOR HOUSE
Clemmons

TANGLEWOOD MANOR HOUSE

The doors at Tanglewood Manor House won't stay locked. "It's because Mr. Will wouldn't put up with a door locked in his house," explained an employee. "And after nightfall, when the lights flicker and go out in the room where he played poker, that's just Mr. Will's prankish way of telling people it's time to go to bed."

Employees of the late Will Reynolds believe that his spirit continues to oversee his 1859 home in Tanglewood Park. That handsome two-story white brick house, now a restaurant with lodging facilities, also retains its original spirit through the country chintz décor. It was this casual atmosphere that Kate and Will Reynolds sought to preserve when they bought and made additions to the house and grounds in the late twenties. Loving the recreation that the lake and woods offered, the Reynoldses built stables and a racetrack, which were used in the training of Reynolds' harness racers. The success of the horses is evidenced by the many trophies remaining on display in the Manor House.

Initially, a sylvan peacefulness draws me to the restaurant, but it is more than tranquility that I find. I feel as if I've come to dinner at a friend's home. As in the days of the Reynoldses, flowers from the rose garden grace every room of the house. Even the food, which is a blend of continental cuisine with Southern overtones, makes me think my host has gone to special pains simply to please me. And the restaurant's staff does go to extra pains. Whether working with the diet of a calorie watcher or of someone with health problems, the staff adapts individual needs to the Manor's five-course menu.

The wine list, offering a range of domestic and imported vintages, has been selected to coordinate with the Manor's choice of three entrées. I particularly like the Marinated Shrimp appetizer, followed by either Chicken Cordon Bleu or Prime Rib. For dessert I am torn between Chocolate Mousse or Black Bottom Pie if they are on the menu. The mousse invariably wins.

In my opinion, dining at the Manor House is the perfect

finale to a day at Tanglewood. Arrive early, then spend the day horseback riding, fishing, swimming, canoeing, or walking through gardens that appear to be a fairy tale come true.

Tanglewood Manor House is located in Tanglewood Park at Clemmons, about ten miles west of Winston-Salem off I-40. Breakfast is served from 6:30 until 9:00 a.m. seven days a week. Dinner is served from 6:00 to 10:00 p.m. Monday through Saturday. For reservations call (919) 766-0591.

TANGLEWOOD MANOR HOUSE'S
MARINATED SHRIMP PORT GIBSON

2½ pounds medium shrimp
½ cup salad oil
¼ cup vinegar
¾ cup minced celery
1¼ tablespoons grated
   onions
½ clove garlic, minced
2½ tablespoons minced
   parsley

2½ tablespoons horseradish
2½ tablespoons Dijon
   mustard
¾ teaspoon salt
⅛ teaspoon pepper
2 tablespoons paprika

Bring a large pot of lightly salted water to a boil; add shrimp. When water comes to a boil again, remove from heat and drain shrimp immediately. Ice down shrimp until cool. Mix all other ingredients and coat shrimp. Marinate overnight. Serves 10 to 12.

TANGLEWOOD MANOR HOUSE'S
RED SNAPPER BOURSIN

Boursin sauce:
½ cup Boursin cheese,
   softened
4 egg yolks

½ cup heavy whipping
   cream

Whip cheese and egg yolks together and set aside. Whip cream and fold into cheese mixture; mix thoroughly. Refrigerate.

Snapper:

4 6-ounce snapper fillets	**3 to 4 shallots, chopped**
2 tablespoons clarified butter	**¼ cup dry vermouth**

Sweat the shallots in skillet of hot clarified butter. Remove shallots; add fillets and cook on one side. Return shallots to pan and cook fillets on remaining side. Remove from pan and place in broiler pan. Deglaze skillet with vermouth and pour over fillets. Coat fillets with Boursin sauce and broil until golden.

May also use deboned chicken that has been pounded thin. Serves 4.

TANGLEWOOD MANOR HOUSE'S
TAR HEEL PIE

Filling:

12 ounces cream cheese, softened	**1½ medium bananas, sliced**
½ cup sugar	**1 9-inch deep-dish pie shell, baked**
½ pint whipping cream	

Mix softened cream cheese with sugar. Whip cream until stiff peaks form. Carefully fold cream into cheese mixture and mix until thoroughly blended. Slice bananas and place in bottom and sides of pie shell. Pour cheese mixture over bananas and chill until firm.

Blueberry glaze:

1 package frozen blueberries	**⅓ cup sugar**
	1 tablespoon cornstarch

Combine ingredients and cook over low heat until thick. Be careful not to break up the berries. Cool to room temperature. Spoon glaze evenly over cheese mixture and chill several house or overnight. Yields 1 pie.

seating
lunch
mon -
sat
seating
dinner
mon - 5 pm
thur 9 pm
fri - 5 pm
sat 10 pm

THE ACADEMY

Salisbury

THE ACADEMY

Do schoolchildren still enjoy their recess period as we used to?

At The Academy, I began with a glass of white wine in a glassed-in garden room that was probably the play area for recess when this quaint restaurant was constructed as the Salisbury Female Academy in 1839. Maxwell Chambers built this sturdy, red brick structure for the First Presbyterian Church, whose property also included a parsonage with enough pasture for a cow. Chambers's will stipulated that the pasture could never be sold by his successors for other purposes. Though this sounds strange today, we have to remember that 130 years ago a cow was important for survival.

Walking through the beautifully restored dining rooms, I had a difficult time deciding on the best place to enjoy dinner. I was relieved that the large blackboard upstairs listed local events instead of algebra problems. I chose a neighboring, cozy dining room with rose-colored floral wallpaper. Their menu is as intriguing as the 1839 curriculum; good old-fashioned recipes are used alongside contemporary ones.

The Academy offers such a wide curriculum that I decided to sample a number of entrées. I gave their Shrimp Creole a high grade for its spicy, almost biting taste, and I discovered that the right formula for Beef Stroganoff contains their exceptional, creamy Worcestershire Sauce. I was sorry that my husband wasn't there to taste the juicy Prime Rib, as he would have awarded it an A-plus. Each entrée is accompanied by a hot loaf of wonderful homemade bread. Later, I learned that the same bread dough is used to wrap the succulent Runza, which became my high scorer.

Desserts have always received high marks with me, so you can imagine what heaven I was in when they brought me their very creamy Cheesecake. Their tasty Cream Cheese German Chocolate Cake is unique thanks to the addition of pecans and coconut. Their Chocolate Pie would please any chocolate lover, but if I were giving grades, then their Gingerbread with Caramel Sauce would go to the head of the class. They were out of their most popular dessert, Butterscotch Pie, so you'll have to order it and tell me about it.

The Academy is located at 115 South Jackson Street in Salisbury. Lunch is served from 11:30 a.m. until 2:30 p.m. Monday through Friday. Dinner is served from 5:00 until 9:00 p.m. Monday through Thursday and from 5:00 until 10:00 p.m. on Friday and Saturday. For reservations call (704) 636-6062.

THE ACADEMY'S RUNZA

Filling:

1 large head of cabbage, chopped	1 cup chopped onion
	salt and pepper to taste
1½ pounds ground beef	

Steam cabbage while browning beef in a skillet. Add onions to beef and sauté until tender. Add cabbage, salt and pepper, cooking over low heat until flavors combine. Let cool slightly.

Dough:

2 packages dry yeast	⅓ cup melted butter
2 cups warm water	1 egg mixed with a dash of water
⅓ cup sugar	
1 tablespoon salt	6 to 8 tablespoons melted butter
5½ cups all-purpose flour	
2 eggs	

Combine yeast, water, sugar, salt and 2 cups of flour in electric mixer and beat for 2 minutes. Add eggs and ⅓ cup melted butter, beating for 1 minute. Beat in remaining 3½ cups of flour with a wooden spoon. Cover mixture with a damp cloth and set in a warm place for 45 to 60 minutes. Punch down dough and let recover and rise again for about 1 hour. Flour a board and separate dough into 6 or 8 equal portions. Roll out portions of dough to size of a saucer, then place 3 tablespoons of cabbage mixture in the center of each. Gather sides of dough and pinch together in the center. Seal by brushing with egg and water mixture. Turn upside down on greased pan and let rise for 10 minutes. Bake in a preheated 375-degree oven for 20 minutes. Pour a tablespoon of melted butter over each and serve. Serves 6 to 8. Note: Runza freezes well.

THE ACADEMY'S
GINGERBREAD WITH CARAMEL SAUCE

Gingerbread:

½ cup butter or margarine	½ teaspoon cloves
¾ cup sugar	1 teaspoon cinnamon
1 cup molasses	1 teaspoon baking soda
1 egg	½ teaspoon salt
2¼ cups all-purpose flour	1 cup hot water
1 teaspoon ginger	

Cream butter and sugar with electric mixer. Add molasses and egg, mixing until combined. Add remaining dry ingredients alternately with water. Pour into a greased 12- by 9-inch pan and bake in a preheated 350-degree oven for 25 to 30 minutes.

Caramel sauce:

1½ cups firmly packed brown sugar	⅛ teaspoon salt
⅔ cup light corn syrup	1 5-ounce can evaporated milk
¼ cup butter	

Combine sugar, syrup and butter in a medium-size saucepan. Cook over medium heat (232 to 240 degrees on a candy thermometer) until mixture begins to thicken, stirring constantly. Remove from heat and stir in salt and milk. Pour over gingerbread and cut into squares. Yields 2¼ cups.

THE LAMPLIGHTER
Charlotte

THE LAMPLIGHTER
A Mediterranean-style house built in 1925 by the Van Ness family has been redecorated to a grandness that would please the flamboyant taste of Mrs. Van Ness. We owe a debt of appreciation to this lady for her reverence for high-quality birch paneling and Doric columns, which remain a part of the interior. The present owners of the house, Woody and Jillian Fox, have taken special care to preserve its intimacy. The warm chocolate brown décor is set off by creatively positioned chandeliers that subtly blink to the passersby.

Before dinner at The Lamplighter, we enjoyed wine at the bar. It is just beyond a marble fireplace that operates year-round, with the aid of an air-conditioning vent in the summer. The wine list is a creative blend of domestic and imported choices, and the restaurant also features a selection of over seventy-five liqueurs.

The menu is varied but leans toward continental cuisine. The Smoked Salmon is an outstanding appetizer, but I've never been known to pass up escargot. Prepared with garlic butter and parsley, it was a true bud teaser. For my main course, I chose scallops. The escargots were complemented, if not excelled, by the delicious fresh scallops. To accompany our meal, a lovely dry Vouvray by Alexis Lichine was perfect. Their wonderful desserts include Chocolate Roulade, Apple-walnut Pie, and assorted flavored cheesecakes. Then my delicious meal culminated with Lamplighter Coffee, which owes a romantic kinship to Irish Coffee.

No, I didn't diet, but I could have ordered any number of broiled fish, chicken, or steak entrées, had I felt the need to do so.

An important charm of this restaurant is its ability to slow down the clock and allow its guests to dine in an unhurried atmosphere. After the liqueur was served, I was astounded to discover that I had been inside this lovely restaurant for over four hours. The relaxed soft glow that The Lamplighter imparts somehow seeps into your being and makes time seem to fall away.

The Lamplighter is located at 1065 East Morehead Street in Charlotte. Dinner is served from 6:30 to 10:00 p.m. nightly. For reservations call (704) 372-5343.

THE LAMPLIGHTER'S
RIBEYE OF VEAL WITH CHANTERELLES

2 tablespoons butter
7 ounces fresh or canned
  chanterelle mushrooms
2 minced shallots
2 ounces brandy
1½ cups veal stock

2 cups heavy cream
salt and pepper to taste
4 tablespoons fresh dill,
  chopped fine
4 8-ounce veal ribeyes

In a skillet, melt butter and sauté mushrooms and shallots until soft. Flame with brandy. Add veal stock and cook until volume is reduced by half. Add cream, bring to a boil, and season with salt and pepper. Add dill and heat through. Grill veal on each side 6 to 7 minutes. Set veal on plates and ladle sauce over top. Serves 4.

THE LAMPLIGHTER'S CHICKEN PECAN

2 large chicken breasts,
  deboned and cut in half
salt and pepper
10 tablespoons butter
3 tablespoons Dijon
  mustard

⅔ cup ground pecans
6 tablespoons vegetable oil
⅔ cup sour cream

Place chicken between two pieces of waxed paper and lightly flatten with a meat mallet. Season with salt and pepper. Melt 6 tablespoons butter in a small pan; remove from heat and whisk in 2 tablespoons mustard. Dip each piece of chicken into mustard mixture and coat heavily with ground pecans. Melt 4 tablespoons butter in a skillet; stir in the oil. When blended and hot, sauté chicken about 4 minutes on each side, or until chicken is cooked. Remove from skillet and keep warm.

Deglaze the skillet with sour cream and whisk the remaining mustard into the sauce. Sauce should retain a strong mustardy flavor. Remove from heat

Present by placing a dollop of the sauce in the middle of a warmed dinner plate and covering dollop with the chicken. Only a small portion of sauce should accompany each piece, in order not to overpower the chicken. Serves 3 to 4.

SPOON'S
Charlotte

SPOON'S   "When people come into an ice cream parlor they are happy, because ice cream is a treat!" says Spoon's current manager. It is an affordable treat, reckoned Whitney Spoon, who began making his ice cream in 1929, at the beginning of the depression. In the early days, Mr. Spoon filled a leather bag with dry ice and ice cream, strapped it to a man's back, sent him out on the street or to ball games to hawk his wares. The popularity of his high-quality ice cream soon allowed Spoon to open his own ice cream parlor.

There have been few changes in Spoon's since the twenties. The sculptured tin ceiling and the tile floor are still there. The only notable change occurred when the new management replaced the old wooden cabinets lining the walls with a graphic design of Charlotte's skyline. The atmosphere remains the same. While having a foot-long hoagy or waiting at the counter for ice cream, you're still apt to see children riding their bikes through the front door or feel a child roller-skating over your foot. You see, adults and children come to Spoon's for the ever-changing variety of ice cream and sherbet, not for the fancy décor. They like it so much that they wait in line on Sundays.

I've been visiting Spoon's for over twenty-two years, and I always choose the double cone because I can get four different scoops of ice cream on it. During my most recent visit, I had their foot-long hoagy. This big hot dog takes on a unique flavor when sliced potatoes, green peppers, and onions are added. It was so filling that I only had room to sample about ten flavors of ice cream.

A taste of each flavor is given on one of those old-fashioned flat wooden spoons. Coconut used to be my favorite, but I have to admit that the strawberry cheesecake beats the competition, with butterscotch chip as the runner-up. My favorite sherbet is the tangerine, but I am also leaning hard toward the raspberry.

I was surprised to learn that adults eat 80 percent of the ice cream at Spoon's. What is the favorite flavor? If you guessed vanilla, you're right.

As children roller-skated past my table, I asked an employee what dieters could eat, and the reply was, "Are you kidding, we don't even carry Sweet'n Low." At Spoon's that's just the way it is—the way it was.

Spoon's is located at Seventh Street and Hawthorne Lane in Charlotte. It is open from 10:00 a.m. until 10:00 p.m. Monday through Saturday, and noon until 10:00 p.m. on Sundays. Reservations are not necessary, but the telephone number is (704) 376-0974.

SPOON'S HOAGY

1 foot-long hot dog bun
2 tablespoons butter
1 tablespoon or more
  mustard
1 foot-long hot dog, cooked
1 tablespoon onion,
  chopped
1 tablespoon green pepper,
  chopped
1 tablespoon sliced potato,
  cooked

Fry hot dog roll in butter until crispy. Spread mustard on both sides of bun and place hot dog inside. Sauté onions, green peppers and potatoes until tender and spread on bun. Serves 1.

SPOON'S BANANA ICE CREAM

4 eggs
2 cups sugar
½ teaspoon salt
2 teaspoons vanilla
1 13-ounce can evaporated
  milk
1 quart heavy cream
2 cups overripe bananas,
  mashed
milk

Beat eggs, slowly adding sugar and salt. Add vanilla, evaporated milk, cream, bananas and enough milk to make 1 gallon; mix thoroughly. Freeze in electric freezer. The trick is to use very brown bananas. Yields 1 gallon.

SPOON'S STRAWBERRY CHEESECAKE ICE CREAM

1 quart buttermilk
2 cups heavy whipping
  cream
1½ cups sugar

2 tablespoons vanilla
  extract
1 jar strawberry topping

Blend first four ingredients thoroughly. Put in freezer unit of refrigerator. Stir well after it begins to freeze and return again to freezer. You can put remixed ingredients in an ice cream maker and use according to machine's directions.

Serve with strawberry topping. Yields 1½ quarts.

ELI'S ON EAST LTD.
Charlotte

ELI'S ON EAST LTD.

Eli's on East Ltd. is in a house that has stood proud in the heart of Charlotte's Dilworth section since 1910. The stunning decoration gives the appearance of someone's ultrachic home rather that a restaurant, but a restaurant it is. The interior of Eli's reminds me of various flavors of sherbet, with their soft but richly colored shades.

Eli's was named after the great-grandfather of its former proprietor, Robert Smoots. Smoots's wife, Karen, wanted to name their restaurant Dolly's of Dilworth because of its modish similarity to the era of *Hello Dolly*, but she was dissuaded when Smoots explained, "All the men will come for the first two weeks, then after they figure out it's only a restaurant, they'll never return."

Of course they would have returned after tasting the French and New American regional cuisine, which is served with great panache under current owners Tony and Dante Dabestani. I mean it's hard not to be dazzled by a Baked Alaska Flambéed in a garden pot with fresh flowers erupting through the meringue. It is equally difficult not to respond to a strolling Dixieland band during brunch on Sunday or to the live piano music from Monday through Saturday nights. This is what makes Eli's a restaurant to put on your list. Reservations are a must for dinner. One man became so frustrated by the restaurant's continuous busy signal that he actually sent a telegram requesting reservations for that evening.

My first visit was for lunch, which is not by reservation. After the taste-teasing Welsh Rarebit appetizer, which was on the house, I "semi-dieted" on the famous Cobb Salad. It is attractively arranged in corn-row strips of chicken, onion, tomatoes, bacon, bleu cheese, and green peas on a bed of lettuce. I chose the House Dressing, which is a pleasing mustard-based vinaigrette blend that perfectly accented the scrumptious salad. The butter-saturated rolls still cause me to salivate just by remembering them, but dessert was the real killer. I couldn't decide between the French-fried Ice Cream and the Peanut Butter Pie, so I splurged on both and was not one bit sorry.

Dinner specialties recommended by friends are Veal Piquant or Stuffed Flounder, but next time I'm going to try the Russian Pavlov Burger, or if calories have gotten the worst of me, I'll happily settle for the fresh fruit served in a huge glass goblet.

I was amused to learn that the green latticework porch and garden were not original to the house. They were added because Charlotte's liquor law forbids people to be seen drinking. No matter; it is a lovely retreat where you may enjoy a sampling from the fine wine list or perhaps the restaurant's unique variation on a Bloody Mary.

I would wish you "Bon appétit," but Eli's is such a delectable adventure, I'll amend that to "Bon voyage!"

Eli's on East Ltd. is located at 311 East Boulevard in Charlotte. Lunch is served from 11:30 a.m. to 2:00 p.m. Dinner is served from 5:30 until 10:00 p.m. Monday through Thursday, from 5:30 until 10:30 p.m. on Friday and Saturday and from 5:30 until 9:00 p.m. on Sunday. Sunday brunch is served from 10:30 a.m. to 2:30 p.m. For reservations call (704) 375-0756 or (704) 375-2969.

ELI'S ON EAST LTD.'S GAZPACHO

4 tomatoes	1 cup red wine vinegar
1 cucumber	½ cup salad oil
1 green pepper	4 teaspoons salt
3 to 4 green onions	¼ teaspoon Tabasco
2 No. 5 cans tomato juice	4 teaspoon Worcestershire
3 cloves garlic, crushed	sauce
¼ cup beef base or 1½ cups beef stock	

In steam kettle or Dutch oven, heat tomato juice to boiling. Peel cucumber and chop with other vegetables. Add the beef base or stock, crushed garlic, and all the vegetables; stir until well mixed. Stir in the vinegar, salad oil, salt, Worcestershire sauce, and Tabasco. Remove from kettle and refrigerate.

Serve with 7 or 8 croutons as a garnish. Serve hot or cold. Yields 1 gallon.

ELI'S ON EAST LTD.'S PEANUT BUTTER PIE

2½ cups milk
1 cup sugar, brown or
   white
⅓ cup or less cornstarch
2 eggs
pinch of salt
1 teaspoon butter

1 cup peanut butter
1 teaspoon vanilla
1 deep 9-inch pie shell,
   baked
whipped cream
chopped peanuts

Bring milk to boiling point. In a bowl, mix sugar, cornstarch, eggs, salt and butter. Slowly stir hot milk into egg mixture. Pour contents of bowl into saucepan and boil a few seconds. Add peanut butter and vanilla and blend well. Pour in piecrust and cool.

Top with whipped cream and peanuts.

ELI'S ON EAST LTD.'S RASPBERRY SOUFFLE

2 envelopes unflavored
   gelatin
½ cup fresh lemon juice
8 eggs, separated
1 cup sugar
1 cup puréed fresh
   raspberries or well-
   drained frozen
   raspberries

4 tablespoons cassis, or 2
   tablespoons brandy and 2
   tablespoons currant jelly
2 cups heavy cream

Prepare a 2-quart soufflé dish with a waxed-paper collar extending 2 to 3 inches above rim of dish. Oil dish and paper.

Soften gelatin in lemon juice and heat over a low flame until light and fluffy. Add raspberries, cassis, and sugar to beaten egg yolks. Add gelatin and cook over hot water until thickened. While mixture cools, beat egg whites until stiff peaks form; whip cream until stiff. Gently fold egg whites into raspberry mixture, then fold in whipped cream. Pour into the soufflé dish and chill.

Remove collar just before serving. Serves 4 to 6.

THE COURTYARD
Matthews

THE COURTYARD

No contemporary builder would recycle the red clay his bulldozer unearthed and bake it into bricks on the site. No, today's builders prefer to haul the dirt away, pay for bricks elsewhere, and haul them back in. But Evard Jefferson Heath and Edward Solomon Reid pursued the old-fashioned, self-sufficient course when they built their general store next to the railroad tracks in Matthews back in 1889. It was the kind of store that my grandmother would have given me a nickel to run over to and buy a spool of thread or some ribbon for my pigtails. Since there wasn't a whole lot of excitement in Matthews, I probably would have tried to get a ride in the town's only elevator.

Today, the structure built by Heath and Reid is called Matthews Mercantile. Entering through the front door, you pass little shops on your way back to The Courtyard. The restaurant has high windows and a country French atmosphere like that of a European cafe. It is, to my taste, prettier than the European cafes that I've seen. Fresh pink carnations grace the mauve linen tablecloths in an intimate blue room that leads to a courtyard banked with bright flowers.

Their Courtyard Muffin is not something you would have come across at the general store, or anywhere else for that matter. Like the bricks that hold this historic building together, they are baked on the site. Served with tangy Apricot Butter, they make it hard to stop with just one. I also sampled their marvelous Strawberry Soup, deep-dish Shrimp Quiche and Combo for lunch. The Combo has three salads—Oriental Chicken, Shrimp and Pasta—plus fresh fruit.

Two dinner entrées I'd heartily recommend are their Swordfish and Salmon. No matter what you order, though, be sure to try one of their fine dessert wines to accent their Chocolate Cake, which is the best I've tasted in a long time.

The Courtyard is located in Matthews Mercantile at 196 North Trade Street in Matthews. Lunch is served from 11:00 a.m. until 3:00 p.m. Monday through Thursday and Saturday. Dinner is served from 6:00 until 9:00 p.m. Tuesday through Thursday and from 6:00 until 10:00 p.m. on Saturday. For reservations call (704) 847-5029.

THE COURTYARD'S CHOCOLATE CAKE

Cake:

1 cup unsifted cocoa	1½ teaspoons vanilla
2 cups water	2¾ cups cake flour
1 cup butter, softened	2 teaspoons baking soda
2½ cups sugar	½ teaspoon salt
4 eggs	½ teaspoon baking powder

Combine cocoa with 1 cup boiling water and whisk until smooth. Add 1 cup cold water and whisk until mixed. Let cool completely. Preheat oven to 350 degrees and grease and flour 3 9-inch cake pans. Cut wax paper to fit pan bottoms. Grease and flour paper. Beat butter, sugar, eggs and vanilla on high speed for 5 minutes until light, scraping often. Sift remaining ingredients together. Add gradually to butter mixture and mix. In separate bowl, alternately add ¼ amounts of the flour mixture with ⅓ amounts of the cocoa mixture, ending with the flour. Bake for 45 minutes.

Filling:

1 cup heavy cream	1½ teaspoons vanilla
¼ cup confectioners sugar	

Beat cream with sugar and vanilla until stiff peaks form. Spread half of filling on first layer and remainder on second layer. Place third layer on top and refrigerate to set.

Frosting:

6 ounces semisweet chocolate	2½ cups confectioners sugar
½ cup milk or light cream	2 cups chopped walnuts
1 cup butter	

Combine chocolate, milk or cream and butter. Stir over medium heat until smooth. Remove from heat and add sugar. Pour mixture into a bowl set over another bowl of ice.

Beat mixture 5 to 6 minutes until it is firm enough to spread. Frost top and sides of cake and cover with walnuts. Yields 1 cake.

THE COURTYARD'S MUFFINS

Muffins:
1/2 cup butter, room
  temperature
3/4 cup sugar
2 eggs, room temperature
3/4 cup sour cream
1 1/2 teaspoons vanilla
1 1/2 cups grated carrots

3/4 cup chopped pecans
2 cups all-purpose flour
1/2 teaspoon salt
1 teaspoon cinnamon
1/4 teaspoon baking soda

Preheat oven to 375 degrees. Grease muffin tins or use paper liners. Cream butter and sugar in electric mixer until fluffy. Beat in eggs one at a time. Blend in sour cream and vanilla. Add carrots and pecans. Sift dry ingredients together and add gradually until incorporated. Do not overmix. Fill tins about 2/3 full and bake for 20 to 25 minutes.

Apricot Butter:
6 to 7 ounces dried
  apricots

2 cups butter, room
  temperature

Place apricots in food processor and process a few seconds. Add butter a bit at a time until mixed. Use with muffins as desired. Yields 12 to 14 muffins.

THE COUNTRY INN
Matthews

THE COUNTRY
INN

What we have come to think of as "country food" is not what is served at The Country Inn. An ancient magnolia tree stands at the entrance of this periwinkle blue farmhouse, which was built in 1890 by William Cecil Black. As the name implies, it has been decorated to resemble an old country inn, with blue-and-white plaid wallpaper. Absent, I am glad to say, are the doodads that some decorators overuse in interiors of this period. On one wall, however, is a cross-stitched motto regarding the importance of family, which I felt was appropriate in this family-operated restaurant. As the restaurant's owner, Ray Lurz, jokingly said, the inn was "my wife's dream and my nightmare." Their daughter works part-time as a waitress, and their son, David, is the chef.

The menu reflects the influence of Lurz's home state in the Maryland-style crabcake. This was a new experience for me, and one that I eagerly recommend. The gold medal, however, has to go to the Mud Pie, which is superb. Dieters should definitely skip the pie and cobblers and take advantage of the vegetarian dish, which contains sautéed mushrooms, peppers, onions and spinach. For dinner you could diet on prime rib, or if not on the calorie wagon, you could choose stuffed shrimp, turkey or a marinated chicken breast. No alcoholic beverages are offered.

My visit was on a late-winter day, and I'm looking forward to returning again in the summer, when that old blue porch is abloom with baskets of geraniums and begonias. Next time I'll opt for the evening hour, when Mrs. Lurz entertains guests by playing old favorites on her piano. Once a youngster told her, "This is gettin' to be my favorite place to eat 'cause I just love your homemade music."

The Country Inn is located at 341 Ames Street in Matthews. Lunch is served from 11:30 a.m. to 2:30 p.m. Tuesday through Friday, and dinner from 5:30 to 8:30 p.m. Tuesday through Saturday. The Sunday buffet is served from noon until 2:00 p.m. For reservations call (704) 847-1447.

THE COUNTRY INN'S
BROILED BARBECUED SHRIMP

1 pound large shrimp,
  shelled and deveined
1/4 cup vegetable oil
1/3 cup chopped onions
1 cup bottled chili sauce
2 tablespoons brown sugar

1/3 cup lemon juice
2 tablespoons
  Worcestershire sauce
2 teaspoons prepared
  mustard
1/2 teaspoon salt

Heat oil and sauté onions until transparent. Add all other ingredients except shrimp; cover and simmer for 10 minutes. Arrange shrimp in foil-lined pan. Pour sauce over shrimp, and broil 3 inches from heat for 5 to 8 minutes. Serves 8.

THE COUNTRY INN'S BAKED BROCCOLI

2 packages frozen chopped
  broccoli
2 eggs, well beaten
1 cup grated medium-sharp
  cheddar cheese

1 can cream of mushroom
  soup
1/3 cup mayonnaise
1 teaspoon onion salt

Cook broccoli. Mix all ingredients together and place in a greased pan. Bake at 350 degrees for 30 minutes or until well set. Serves 6 to 8.

THE COUNTRY INN'S OVEN-CRISP CHICKEN

4 chicken breasts, deboned
1/4 cup sour cream
1 1/4 teaspoon lemon juice
1/2 teaspoon garlic salt
3/4 teaspoon celery salt
salt and pepper

1 teaspoon Worcestershire
  sauce
1 teaspoon paprika
1 cup herb-seasoned
  stuffing mix
1/4 cup butter, melted

Mix sour cream, lemon juice and seasonings. Dip chicken into mixture and roll in stuffing mix. Arrange chicken in greased shallow baking dish. Brush with melted butter. Bake uncovered at 350 degrees for 1 hour or until done. Serves 4.

THE COUNTRY INN'S CRAB CAKES

1 pound back fin crabmeat
  (pick out shells carefully)
2 slices bread
¼ cup milk
¼ teaspoon salt
1 egg, beaten
1 teaspoon Old Bay
  Seasoning

1 tablespoon mayonnaise
1 tablespoon Worcestershire
  sauce
1 tablespoon chopped
  parsley
2 tablespoon margarine

Remove crusts from bread and break bread into small pieces; moisten with milk. Mix all ingredients except margarine, and shape into large, flat cakes. Fry in margarine until light brown on both sides. Serves 4 to 6.

PINE CREST INN
Tryon

PINE CREST INN

Thanksgiving is a time for expressing thanks for our families and our good fortune. The Pine Crest Inn celebrates Thanksgiving by participating in the Tryon-area's festival of the hunt, which includes a "blessing of the hounds." This event came into being some time after 1917, when Carter Brown of Holland, Michigan, purchased the 1906 inn, which had originally been a sanatorium, and converted it into an equestrian winter haven. Brown initiated all manner of horse shows and steeplechase and fox-hunting events. The reins of the inn have passed into the able hands of Bob Johnson, but the inn's theme remains equine. The casual lobby plays host to art shows in which horses are frequently portrayed in paintings and sculptures. Other shows feature ceramics and woven wear.

Inside their rustic dining room with its free-form wooden tables, I sipped their wonderful mountain water while enjoying their fresh Herbed Tomato Soup. The quality of the summer tomatoes and fresh herbs combined to give this soup a vaguely meaty taste which was most enjoyable. I continued with their Orange Roughy seasoned with herbs and bread crumbs. Their technique elevates this rather inexpensive and often overlooked fish into better standing. Bob Johnson, it should be noted, has compiled an extensive wine list featuring excellent lesser-known brands at lower than typical cost.

For dessert, their old-fashioned Spiced Crumb Pudding provided a good balance with my daughter Daintry's Blackened Red Snapper as well as with Bob's Salmon with Dill Mousseline Sauce. I chose their fantastic Chocolate Truffle Torte.

I never sleep as well elsewhere as I do in the mountains, and our comfy, rustic bedroom with its fireplace was no exception. The dining room takes on a different, welcoming personality in the morning. A breakfast specialty is waffles with a unique topping I had to get in case you can't get away to this warm and vital inn right away.

Pine Crest Inn is located at 200 Pine Crest Lane in Tryon. Breakfast is served from 8:00 until 9:30 a.m. Monday through Friday and from 8:00 until 10:00 a.m. on Saturday and Sunday. Lunch is served from 11:30 a.m. until 2:00 p.m. Monday through Saturday and from noon until 2:00 p.m. on Sunday. Dinner is served from 6:00 until 8:30 p.m. Sunday through Thursday and from 6:00 until 9:00 p.m. on Friday and Saturday. For reservations call (704) 859-9135.

PINE CREST INN'S WAFFLE TOPPING

6 tart apples, peeled, cored
   and sliced
2 cups pecan halves
1 teaspoon vanilla

¼ teaspoon ground
   cinnamon
dash of nutmeg
maple syrup

Place apples, pecans, vanilla, cinnamon and nutmeg in a large saucepan. Add enough maple syrup to cover. Simmer on low heat for 20 minutes, stirring frequently. Serves 10 or more.

PINE CREST INN'S ORANGE ROUGHY

½ teaspoon ground basil
½ teaspoon ground
   rosemary
½ teaspoon thyme
½ teaspoon tarragon
salt and pepper to taste

1 cup bread crumbs
1 egg
1 tablespoon milk or water
2 6-ounce orange roughy
   fillets
2 tablespoons butter

Combine basil, rosemary, thyme, tarragon, salt and pepper with bread crumbs and spread out on a dish. Beat egg with milk or water in a shallow bowl. Dip fish into egg wash and place in bread crumbs, making sure that both sides are well-coated. Melt butter in a sauté pan and sauté fish 3 to 4 minutes on each side. Serve with wild rice and garnish with parsley and sliced fruit. Serves 2.

PINE CREST INN'S SPICED CRUMB PUDDING

Pudding:

1½ cups soft bread crumbs
1 cup buttermilk
3 tablespoons softened
   butter (no substitute)
1 cup brown sugar
2 tablespoons molasses

½ teaspoon sifted flour
½ teaspoon salt
1 teaspoon soda
½ teaspoon cinnamon
⅛ teaspoon cloves
½ cup raisins

Combine bread crumbs and buttermilk. In a separate bowl, mix butter, brown sugar and molasses until thoroughly combined. Stir into bread-crumb mixture. Sift flour, salt, soda, cinnamon and cloves together and stir into mixture. Blend in raisins. Pour into a greased 10-by-6-by-2-inch loaf pan and bake in a preheated 350-degree oven for 45 to 50 minutes.

Satin Sauce:

½ cup butter
1 cup confectioners sugar
1 beaten egg

4 tablespoons fresh-
   squeezed lemon juice

Melt butter in top of a double boiler over simmering water. Add sugar and stir until mixture thickens and sugar dissolves. Stir in egg. Remove from heat and cool. Add lemon juice, stirring until incorporated. Pour sauce over pudding and serve. Serves 4 to 6.

ECHO MOUNTAIN INN
Hendersonville

ECHO MOUNTAIN INN

An unknown, early gourmet believed that a good dining experience should involve all the senses, and so the clinking of glasses in a toast was instituted in order to satisfy the auditory sense. One has to wonder if the Patterson family, who built their flagstone home in 1896, purposely positioned the structure so they could hear the messages they hollered across the mountain returned. Current inn owner Marion Mulford doesn't know whether it has something to do with increased mountain foliage or ecological changes, but echoes can no longer be heard here. "But," she added, "the acoustics on this mountain are unbelievable!" I followed her through the gracious living room, where a group of lady quilters was meeting for lunch, and out onto the dining porch with its appealing view of Hendersonville, some three miles away. Sure enough, seated at one end of the porch, I could hear guests at the other end perfectly.

After the home was the Pattersons' residence, it became a girls' camp named Camp Happiness before it was turned into an inn by the eccentric Mrs. Royall in the 1930s. Mrs. Royall was quite particular about her clientele. She was extremely frank in interviewing prospective guests. She served them with her good china, crystal and silver, and she wanted to make sure that these special services weren't wasted on unappreciative people. Innkeepers Richard and Marion Mulford were as amused by Mrs. Royall's approach as I was, but after spending the night in one of their beautiful country-style bedrooms overlooking the Blue Ridge Mountains, hiking around the mountain and taking a dip in the pool, I thought an interview for admission might not be too hard to handle. And that was before I had lunch.

The haze was burning off the mountain as I ordered Chilled Apple Soup. Like so many good local recipes, this one was created out of a desire to make something delicious using native apples. Then came my Chicken Supreme, a tasty medley of chicken salad, one-fourth of a fresh pineapple and a variety of other fresh fruits, served with a croissant. If it's on the menu when you visit, do order the Ricotta

Torte with Strawberries. It's so light that it slips down as easily as the tension-filled world slips away on Echo Mountain.

Echo Mountain Inn is located at 2849 Laurel Park Highway near Hendersonville. Lunch is served from 11:30 a.m. until 2:00 p.m. Tuesday through Saturday. Dinner is served from 6:00 p.m. until 8:30 p.m. Tuesday through Sunday. The Sunday brunch buffet is served from 11:30 a.m. until 2:00 p.m. Continental breakfast is served to lodging guests. For reservations call (704) 693-9626.

ECHO MOUNTAIN INN'S
RICOTTA TORTE WITH STRAWBERRIES

Pastry:

3 cups ricotta cheese	¼ teaspoon almond extract
1 cup sugar	2 tablespoons plain flour
3 eggs	

Place cheese and sugar in electric mixing bowl and whip on high for 4 minutes. Add eggs and whip for 2 minutes; add almond extract and fold in flour until well-mixed. Pour mixture into 2 paper-lined, buttered and floured 8-inch cake pans and bake in a preheated 350-degree oven for 30 to 35 minutes. Remove and cool.

French Almond Pastry Cream:

1 cup whipping cream	1 egg white, stiffly beaten
2 tablespoons confectioners sugar	2 ounces semisweet chocolate, shaved
1 teaspoon almond extract or almond liqueur	

Whip the cream with an electric mixer until stiff peaks form. Add sugar slowly, folding in gently. Add extract or liqueur slowly. Fold in egg white until completely incorporated. Spread cream between pastry layers and over top and sides. Add shaved chocolate to sides.

French Apricot Glaze:

1 cup apricot jam	**¾ cup extra-fine sugar**
1¼ cups water	**½ pint sliced strawberries**

Combine jam, water and sugar in a small saucepan and cook over medium heat until jam is dissolved, stirring constantly. Bring slowly to a rolling boil and cook until thickened. Strain through a sieve and cool. Place strawberries on top of torte and spread glaze over strawberries. Yields 1 torte.

ECHO MOUNTAIN INN'S
CHILLED APPLE SOUP

6 Red Delicious apples	**½ cup sugar**
½-inch stick of cinnamon	**¼ cup lemon juice**
3 tablespoons lemon juice	**½ cup black currant jelly**
½ peel of a lemon, coarsely	**salt to taste**
grated	**ground cinnamon to taste**
1 quart Beaujolais	**6 tablespoons sour cream**

Peel apples and cut into thin slices. Place in saucepan with cinnamon stick, 3 tablespoons lemon juice and lemon peel and cook over medium heat until juice is absorbed. Remove cinnamon stick. Purée apple mixture coarsely in a food processor. Put mixture into a bowl and add wine, sugar, ¼ cup lemon juice, jelly, salt and cinnamon, mixing thoroughly. Cover and refrigerate until completely chilled. Serve with a tablespoon of sour cream per portion. Serves 6.

HIGH HAMPTON INN
Cashiers

HIGH HAMPTON INN

After sitting for a bit on the back porch balcony at High Hampton Inn, a feeling of serenity begins to permeate your being. Initially, however, the view of Hampton Lake curled at the base of Rock and Chimney Top mountains elicits an emotion no less than exhilaration.

Spectacles always make me hungry, so when I went through the luncheon buffet I helped myself to generous portions of Spanish Eggplant, corned beef and cabbage, corn relish, macaroni salad, a green salad, several sausage bread muffins, and lemonade.

There are so many activities at this family-style inn—including tennis, golf, swimming, skeet shooting, fishing, and canoeing—that there is ample opportunity to burn calories. But if rocking on the porch is your definition of exercise, as it often is mine, then take advantage of the salads and fresh melon selections for lunch and concentrate on broiled fish at the dinner buffet. I must point out, however, that you would miss the inn's special dessert, Black Bottom Pie, which would be a true deprivation.

The present structure at High Hampton was built in 1922 by E. L. McKee, the grandfather of the present owner. However, the socializing there dates back to 1791, when Wade Hampton, the Confederate general and South Carolina governor, built his retreat in the Cashiers valley. He was not the only prominent figure to own the property; his daughter Caroline married Dr. William Steward Halstead, who was head of Johns Hopkins Hospital and is credited with inventing rubber surgical gloves, localized anesthesia, and a surgical technique that is still practiced in some hospitals.

Caroline much preferred the unpretentious life of supervising the landscaping of her dahlia garden at High Hampton to the society life of Baltimore. Dahlias continue to be nurtured at the inn, and they provide a cheerful addition to the bucolic surroundings.

High Hampton Inn is located on N.C. 107, two miles south of Cashiers. It is open daily from April 1 to November 1, and from Wednesday through Sunday during the week of Thanksgiving. Breakfast is served from 7:00 to 9:30 a.m.; lunch from 12:15 to 2:15 p.m.; and dinner from 6:30 to 8:15 p.m. The Rocky Mountain Lounge is open from 6:00 until 8:00 p.m. For reservations call (704) 743-2411.

HIGH HAMPTON INN'S BLACK BOTTOM PIE

Crust:

1½ cups crushed zwieback	6 tablespoons melted butter
¼ cup powdered sugar	1 teaspoon cinnamon

Mix all ingredients well and pat out evenly into a deep 9-inch pie pan. Bake 300 degrees for 15 minutes. Cool.

Chocolate filling:

1 tablespoon gelatin	4 teaspoons cornstarch
¼ cup cold water	½ teaspoon vanilla
2 cups half-and-half	1½ ounces chocolate,
4 egg yolks (reserve whites)	melted
1 cup sugar	

Soak gelatin in cold water. Scald half-and-half. Beat egg yolks, and add sugar and cornstarch. Place in double boiler and stir half-and-half in gradually; keep stirring until custard coats a spoon, about 20 minutes. Remove from heat and pour out 1 cup of custard. Add chocolate to cup of custard and beat until well blended and cool. Add vanilla and pour into pie shell. Add gelatin to remaining custard; cool, but do not allow to stiffen.

To complete custard filling:

3 egg whites	¼ cup sugar
¼ teaspoon salt	1 teaspoon almond extract
¼ teaspoon cream of tartar	

Make stiff meringue by beating egg whites with salt until frothy. Add cream of tartar and beat until stiff enough to hold a peak, then gradually beat in sugar until very stiff. While remaining custard is still soft, fold in meringue very gently, blend in almond extract, and chill. Pour over chocolate custard.

Topping:

| 1 cup heavy whipping cream | 2 tablespoons powdered sugar |

Whip the cream, add powdered sugar, and spread over top of pie. Chill until served.

HIGH HAMPTON INN'S SPANISH EGGPLANT

1 large eggplant	4 tablespoons Parmesan cheese
1 teaspoon salt	1 teaspoon salt, or to taste
4 tablespoons butter	$\frac{1}{2}$ teaspoon or more white pepper
$\frac{1}{2}$ cup chopped onions	
$\frac{1}{2}$ cup chopped green peppers	$\frac{1}{2}$ teaspoon garlic powder or salt
1 $14\frac{1}{2}$-ounce can tomatoes	
$\frac{1}{4}$ cup brown sugar	$\frac{1}{2}$ cup bread crumbs

In a saucepan dissolve 1 teaspoon salt in a pint of water. Peel and cube eggplant and parboil in salted water. In separate skillet melt 2 tablespoons butter and sauté onions and peppers; set aside. Drain eggplant and tomatoes and mix together in greased casserole. Season with brown sugar, 2 tablespoons Parmesan cheese, salt, pepper and garlic. Add onions and peppers and mix thoroughly. Melt remaining butter and drizzle over bread crumbs. Sprinkle crumbs and remaining cheese over vegetables. Bake at 350 degrees for 35 to 40 minutes or until brown. Serves 4.

THE CENTRAL HOUSE RESTAURANT/
OLD EDWARDS INN
Highlands

**THE CENTRAL
HOUSE RESTAURANT/
OLD EDWARDS INN**   In 1875, two Kansans named Kelsey and Hutchinson studied a map of the United States, trying to decide the best location for a new town they planned to build. They drew one line from Chicago to Savannah and another from Baltimore to New Orleans. The two lines intersected at a point in North Carolina near its borders with South Carolina and Georgia.

Kelsey and Hutchinson predicted that the intersection would one day mark the exact center of population of the eastern United States, and that a town built on that spot would become a great commercial center.

Even though the location proved to be on an elevated mountain plateau in the middle of rugged hill country, Kelsey and Hutchinson were not deterred. They purchased an eight-hundred-acre tract, laid out a town, and began sending advertisements all over the country glorifying their new town, Highlands.

The Old Edwards Inn and the adjoining Central House Restaurant were two of the first structures in the new town. The Old Edwards Inn was built in 1878 and has been in continuous operation since that time. The Central House Restaurant began as a separate hotel in 1878, but the two buildings are now connected as one establishment. Rip and Pat Benton purchased them both in 1982 and have made extensive renovations.

In deciding how to restore the two buildings, the Bentons chose the wholesome country charm of the early rough-and-tumble frontier town. They brought in a master stenciler, who found stencils authentic to the frontier days. They also chose paints and wall coverings authentic to the Colonial period. To complement the establishment's new look, they added some of the best pieces of furniture from their own antique business.

The Bentons brought many years of experience as restaurateurs to their new location. For sixteen years, they have owned Blanche's Courtyard Restaurant on St. Simons Island. The exceptional seafood dishes that dominate the

Central House's dinner menu attest to the culinary expertise they have gained in their years off the Georgia coast.

The Bentons return to Blanche's Courtyard each winter, and the inn and restaurant in Highlands are therefore closed at the end of November. But the Bentons return, as do the tourists. Each spring, the Highlands locations reopen the first week in April.

The Central House Restaurant in the Old Edwards Inn is located on Main Street in Highlands. It is open from the first week in April until the end of November. Lunch is served every day but Sunday from 11:30 a.m. to 2:30 p.m; dinner is served every night from 5:00 to 9:30 p.m. Breakfast is served to inn guests only. For reservations call (704) 526-5036.

CENTRAL HOUSE RESTAURANT'S
APPLE CAKE

3 eggs
2 cups sugar
1 cup oil
2 cups plain flour
2 teaspoons cinnamon
$\frac{1}{2}$ teaspoon nutmeg
   (optional)
$\frac{1}{4}$ teaspoon allspice
   (optional)

1 teaspoon baking soda
$\frac{1}{2}$ teaspoon salt
1 teaspoon vanilla
1 cup chopped walnuts
5 cups tart apples, pared
   and sliced thin

Beat eggs until thick and light. Combine sugar and oil. Add to eggs with mixer on medium speed. Stir together flour, spices, baking soda and salt. Add to egg mixture. Add vanilla. Beat mixture, stirring in nuts. Spread apples in buttered 13- by 9-inch pan. Pour batter over apples, spreading to cover. Bake at 350 degrees for 1 hour or until toothpick comes out clean. Serve warm topped with vanilla ice cream and lemon sauce.

CENTRAL HOUSE RESTAURANT'S
LEMON SAUCE

2 cups water
1 cup sugar
2 tablespoons cornstarch
1/4 teaspoon salt
1 egg yolk

1/4 cup lemon juice
1/4 teaspoon grated lemon
    rind
4 tablespoons butter

Place water in saucepan and bring to a boil. Mix together sugar, cornstarch and salt. Dissolve mixture with small amount of boiling water, whipping gently with a wire whip. Cook until thickened and clear. Beat egg yolk and lemon juice together in small bowl. Add slowly to thickened mixture, whipping constantly. Keep hot only the amount of sauce needed. If kept hot too long, sauce will thin. Remove from heat, add lemon rind and butter, and blend thoroughly. Store in covered container in refrigerator. Serve warm over any kind of cobbler. Yields 2 cups.

CENTRAL HOUSE RESTAURANT'S
SOUTHERN SPOONBREAD

1 cup self-rising cornmeal
3 cups milk
2 tablespoons shortening

3 eggs
2 tablespoons sugar

Mix cornmeal, 2 cups of the milk and shortening in a large, heavy pot. Bring to a boil, stirring constantly, since mixture will stick and scorch very quickly. Remove from heat. Combine eggs, remaining cup of milk and sugar in separate bowl. Mix well. Add egg mixture to hot cornmeal mixture and mix well. Pour into well-greased 1 1/2-quart casserole. Bake at 400 degrees for 30 to 40 minutes. (If you need to bake it more quickly, put less batter in the casserole.) When done, center should be firm and top should be golden brown. Serves 6 to 8.

JARRET HOUSE
Dillsboro

JARRETT HOUSE The first words I overheard upon entering the dining room of Jarrett House were, "I could make a whole meal out of these biscuits alone." Sampling one of the biscuits before my fresh rainbow trout arrived, I agreed with the biscuit lover, but then I didn't do too badly with the candied apples, green beans, beets, potatoes, coleslaw, and iced tea sweetened with honey. All around me I heard acclamations for the peach cobbler, but Jim Hartbarger, the inn's owner and former college basketball coach, said I should try the vinegar pie. I must admit the name puts you off, but I assure you the taste will not. It was, as his wife, Jean, described it, like a pecan pie without the pecans. Don't think that decalorizes it; there's no such thing as a low-calorie meal at Jarrett House.

Although I would definitely again order the trout, which is fresh from a neighboring hatchery, you might prefer the country ham or fried chicken in "all you can stuff" quantities.

The 1884 house will bring back childhood memories of stuffing yourself at Grandma's. It has been "prettied up" a bit by the Hartbargers, but they have been careful not to disturb its quaint atmosphere. The Victorian-style parlor still looks as if my grandmother should be rocking beneath the lace wall hanging with the Twenty-third Psalm on it. The three-story rambling white structure, built by the man for whom Dillsboro was named, is encircled with wrought iron porches. The turn-of-the-century traveler could get a bed and feed for his horse for twenty-five cents. Meals were a dime extra. Later the inn was sold to Jarrett, who cured hams upstairs and in the basement near the natural sulphur spring produced a concoction that neighbors said smelled peculiarly like alcohol. That was not the only scandal to come out of the house. During the roar of the twenties two young ladies from Edenton are reported to have shocked half the town when they lit up cigarettes right on the front porch.

The inn is in a dry county, but brown bagging is permitted. The guests partake of refreshment in the upstairs lounge, but for some reason never feel comfortable bringing their brown bags downstairs to the dining room.

You'll enjoy the food, and if you have the opportunity to sleep in one of the bedrooms furnished with antiques and lacking the cumbersome paraphernalia of telephones and television, then you'll relax right into the spirit, especially with the mountains nestling right behind the inn's back door.

Jarrett House is located at the intersection of U.S. 23 Business and U.S. 441 south in Dillsboro. Breakfast is served from 7:00 to 9:30 a.m., lunch from 11:30 a.m. to 2:00 p.m., and dinner from 5:00 to 8:30 p.m., daily from April through October. For reservations call (704) 586-9964.

JARRETT HOUSE'S PICKLED BEETS

1 onion	½ cup vinegar
1 can beets	1 cup sugar

Slice onion thin. Mix in a bowl with beets, juice, vinegar and sugar. Cover and refrigerate for several hours or overnight. Serves 4 to 6.

JARRETT HOUSE'S SQUASH CASSEROLE

1 pound squash, fresh or canned	5 or 6 leftover biscuits, crumbled fine, or corn bread
1 medium onion, chopped	salt and pepper
6 slices bacon, cooked and crumbled	3 to 4 tablespoons melted butter

Cook squash until almost tender. Drain and place in greased flat, ovenproof pan. Add onions, bacon, and crumbled biscuits on top. Pour melted butter over biscuits. Bake at 350 degrees for 30 minutes, or until golden brown. Serves 4.

JARRETT HOUSE'S VINEGAR PIE

½ cup margarine, melted
2 tablespoons flour
2 tablespoons vinegar
1½ cups sugar

1 tablespoon vanilla extract
3 eggs
1 9-inch pie shell, unbaked

Combine first six ingredients, blending well. Pour into pie shell. Bake at 300 degrees for 45 minutes.

RANDOLPH HOUSE
Bryson City

RANDOLPH HOUSE   As your old oak rocker shuttles back and forth on the front porch of Randolph House, the flicker of the evening's fireflies is accompanied by the sound of crickets. This house, listed on the National Register of Historic Places, was once called Peaceful Lodge, and with good reason.

No one races to keep up with schedules here. There are no clocks, radios, or televisions; changes in time are marked by the varying aromas issuing from Ruth Adams' kitchen. The morning is signaled by the scent of bacon and coffee (which will accompany eggs, grits, sweet rolls, and jam that was made in the summer kitchen.) Dinner is announced by the summoning smell of angel biscuits.

That heavenly fragrance led my daughter Heather and me from our rocking chairs on the porch and into the antique-filled dining room of Randolph House. The residents of Bryson City called this "mansion on the hill" when the house was constructed in 1895. The house was built by lumber tycoon Amos Frye and his wife, Lillian, the town's first practicing female attorney. Being an enterprising couple, the Fryes used their mansion not only to entertain guests, but also as a lodge and a gift shop.

As was the custom of the day, Mrs. Frye's unmarried sister, Eugenia Rowe, lived with the family. She was an accomplished artist schooled in the Flemish tradition. In the lobby of the inn is Eugenia's rendition of Adam and Eve fleeing the Garden of Eden. Because Eve's filmy dress is inching "indecently" up her thigh, Eugenia became known about town as an eccentric. Consequently, she spent many of her years alone in the attic, painting her visions. In a painting that hung across from me at dinner, grapes glistened so deliciously that I wanted to pick them.

Instead, I drank my dry white wine, a Wente Pinot Chardonnay, which was a perfect accompaniment for my delicious Veal Scallopini. Obviously, Mrs. Adams' food is not strictly Southern. Even though Heather ate every bite of her very Southern fried chicken, the cuisine is heavily influenced by gourmet fare of other parts of the world. The wonderful

Poppy Seed Torte with Raspberry Sauce is an excellent case in point. This dish is not exactly a calorie cutter, but Mrs. Adams is happy to prepare something to suit your diet if she is given adequate advance notice.

Randolph House is located in Bryson City on Fryemont Road. From Asheville follow I-40 west to U.S. 19A-23, and take the second Bryson City exit. Breakfast is served from 8:00 to 9:30 a.m., and dinner from 6:00 to 8:00 p.m., daily from April through October. For reservations call (704) 488-3472.

RANDOLPH HOUSE'S POPPY SEED TORTE

Pastry:

1/3 cup poppy seeds	2 cups cake flour, sifted
3/4 cup milk	2 1/2 teaspoons baking
3/4 cup butter	powder
1 1/2 cups sugar	1/4 teaspoon salt
1 1/2 teaspoons vanilla	4 egg whites, stiffly beaten

Soak seeds in milk for one hour. Cream butter and sugar in electric mixer until fluffy. Mix in vanilla, milk and seeds. Sift together remaining dry ingredients and stir into creamed mixture. Fold in egg whites. Bake in four well-greased and lightly floured round cake pans, making very thin layers. Bake at 375 degrees for 15 to 20 minutes. Cool and remove from pans.

Filling:

1/2 cup sugar	4 egg yolks, slightly beaten
1 tablespoon cornstarch	1 teaspoon vanilla
1 1/2 cups milk	1/4 cup chopped walnuts

Mix sugar and cornstarch. Combine milk and egg yolks, and stir gradually into sugar mixture. Cook, stirring, until bubbly. Cool. Add vanilla and walnuts to mixture. Spread filling between layers of pastry. Chill 2 to 3 hours, then sift confectioners sugar on top. Serve with raspberry sauce (see recipe below).

RANDOLPH HOUSE'S RASPBERRY SAUCE

1 package frozen
  raspberries
¾ cup sugar

1 tablespoon cornstarch
1 tablespoon butter

Combine all ingredients in a saucepan and cook over medium heat until slightly thickened. Chill and serve over poppy seed torte.

RANDOLPH HOUSE'S ANGEL BISCUITS

1½ packages dry yeast
3 tablespoons warm water
5 cups self-rising flour
¼ cup sugar

¼ teaspoon salt
1½ cups shortening
2½ cups buttermilk

Combine yeast and warm water; let stand five minutes. Combine dry ingredients in large bowl; cut in shortening until mixture resembles coarse crumbs. Add buttermilk to yeast mixture and mix with dry ingredients. Beat vigorously. Cover; let rise for two hours. Beat dough again. Cut and fill greased muffin tins half-full, and let rise to double size. Bake at 450 degrees for 7 to 10 minutes. Yield about 60 biscuits. Dough will keep in refrigerator for about a week.

THE GROVE PARK INN
AND COUNTRY CLUB
Asheville

THE GROVE PARK INN AND COUNTRY CLUB

The wind, for some reason, feels cleaner when it greets you on the high balcony of The Grove Park Inn and Country Club. Perhaps blowing through the blue haze of the Smoky Mountains gives it a certain crispness. I don't know, but I can say that looking across at the mountains, with the city of Asheville tucked below, makes the word spectacular seem inadequate.

E. W. Grove must have had a similar attitude when he built this inn in 1913. Even today it is awesome to walk through the solid granite structure, which was literally hewed out of Sunset Mountain. Grove's philosophy of "thinking big" was part of his desire to create a hotel that would be considered the epitome of gracious hospitality. The original advertising for the inn proudly stated that "All our waiters wear freshly laundered white gloves," and "Guests are encouraged to speak in low tones." Grove Park was billed not as a sanatorium, but as "a resting place for tired people." Having just completed a long drive on one of my restaurant tours, I was the perfect applicant when I arrived there.

I lunched in the Sunset Terrace, and I can't imagine either the food or the service being better. I had a delicious cup of French onion soup and a bouquet of fresh fruits served with a special yogurt-based dressing. What a scrumptious way to sabotage the calories! Though the dessert tray of French pastries was intriguing, I bravely passed up those enticements. A complete beer and wine list is available for both lunch and dinner. It features premium selections of California wines, plus domestic and imported beers.

There are six separate restaurants at the inn and country club, each featuring a distinct atmosphere. It was originally suggested that "Gentlemen not desiring to dine in evening dress may use the East dining room." Today, the inn's requirements of guests are not so stringent, but its self-imposed requirements for good food have not been relaxed.

An appetizing way to begin your meal is with the Marinated Herring. My personal choice would be to follow with the Fillet of Sole Poached in Champagne, but I'm told that the established winner is a generous cut of Prime Rib, with the Veal Oscar as a close runner-up.

After dining, it's entertaining to read the inscriptions etched into the huge fireplaces at either end of the lobby. Each is large enough to burn twelve-foot logs. Chiseled into the stones are the thoughts of Emerson, Thoreau, and Jefferson, and a few quotes that strain one's Latin to translate. But the philosophical inscription that seemed best suited to the era of The Grove Park Inn and Country Club was "Be not simply good, be good for something!"

The Grove Park Inn and Country Club is located on Macon Street in Asheville. Serving hours for breakfast, lunch, and dinner vary at each of the six restaurants. For reservations call (704) 252-2711.

THE GROVE PARK INN AND COUNTRY CLUB'S
ESCALLOPS OF VEAL

1½ pounds linguine
½ cup pine nuts
6 6-ounce veal medallions, cut from leg*
salt and pepper to taste
plain flour
½ cup butter
1 cup sliced chanterelles or shitake mushrooms

juice from 1 lemon
1 tablespoon brandy
½ cup white wine
1 cup heavy whipping cream
¼ cup water
1 tablespoon cornstarch
2 teaspoons fresh parsley, chopped

Boil linguine for 6 to 8 minutes until barely tender and still crisp inside. Set aside and keep warm. Toast pine nuts for about 8 minutes until light brown. Set aside. Pound veal until flat. Salt and pepper veal and dust lightly with flour on both sides. Melt butter in a large sauté pan and brown veal on both sides. Add mushrooms and lemon juice and stir to combine. Stir in brandy, wine and cream until mixture is well incorporated. Mix water with cornstarch and stir into sauce, stirring until sauce thickens slightly. Place pasta on warmed plates and ladle sauce over top. Place veal on plates and ladle remainder of sauce over veal. Garnish with pine nuts and parsley. Serves 6.

*Use scallopini or chops if medallions are unavailable.

THE GROVE PARK INN AND COUNTRY CLUB'S
SEAFOOD IMPERIAL

$^1/_2$ cup sesame oil
18 shrimp
$1^1/_2$ pounds grouper, cut
  into cubes
$^1/_2$ cup scallions, minced
$^1/_2$ cup carrots, chopped fine
$^1/_2$ cup celery, chopped fine
1 cup Chinese cabbage,
  shredded
$^1/_2$ cup shitake mushrooms,
  sliced thin

$^1/_2$ cup whole water
  chestnuts
1 cup snow peas
$^1/_2$ cup Chinese rice wine
1 cup chicken stock
1 tablespoon oyster sauce
1 tablespoon soy sauce
salt and pepper to taste
1 tablespoon cornstarch
$^1/_4$ cup water

In a large sauté pan, heat oil on medium-high and sauté shrimp, scallops and grouper. Add scallions, carrots, celery, cabbage, mushrooms, water chestnuts and snow peas. When fish and vegetables are barely tender, stir in wine and chicken stock and bring to a boil. Lower heat and season with oyster sauce, soy sauce and salt and pepper. Stir cornstarch into water and let dissolve. Add cornstarch to seafood mixture and stir until mixture thickens. Place on plates and garnish with scallions, if desired. Serves 8 to 10.

5 BOSTON WAY
Asheville

5 BOSTON WAY

Build a village of homes before building your own home? A novel approach, and one you're unlikely to see today. But that was part of George Vanderbilt's grand design for Biltmore Estate in the late 1880s. The home at 5 Boston Way was part of the original Biltmore Village that Vanderbilt ordered constructed for the skilled artisans who were to build Biltmore. The homes were located near the railroad built for transporting materials to the mansion's site. The Biltmore Village homes weren't of today's temporary type; they were built, as things were back then, to last. The appealing home at 5 Boston Way is reminiscent of the English style of building. It features a rough stucco exterior called pebble-dash construction. It was completed around 1901 and was leased to one of the artisans for the duration of the mansion's construction. Most of the village's buildings were sold after Vanderbilt's death, and in 1979 this charming area was declared a historic district. Other houses in the village have been converted into interesting shops and boutiques.

On the sunny day that I revisited the restaurant, new proprietors Linda Fish and Ed Horgan had just finished their own transformation of 5 Boston Way. Today, it has a casual yet upscale setting that retains strong traces of an English country cottage. The inspirational use of color brightens both dining rooms and adds a cheerful note to the lounge. The sun was streaming through the windows and skylights, which further accented the bright décor, but at night the cozy fireplace and soft glow of candlelight communicates a more intimate ambience.

For lunch I chose polar opposites—a very Southern dish called Chicken Old Virginia, which is a kind of jazzy cordon bleu that substitutes grits for cheese and is accented by a wonderful Peanut Sauce, and an innovative entrée called Salmon Fillet with Warm Tartar Sauce. This dish utilizes Southern techniques and ingredients that make it melt in your mouth.

I thought I had tasted cheesecake in every possible variation, but their Southern Comfort Cheesecake makes imaginative use of a favorite and famous Southern drink. You're going to like it, just as I liked the new cuisine and décor.

As its name suggests, the restaurant is located at 5 Boston Way in Asheville. Lunch is served from 11:30 a.m. until 2:30 p.m. and dinner from 5:30 until 10:00 p.m. Monday through Saturday. Sunday dinner is served from 6:00 until 9:00 p.m. For reservations call (704) 274-1111.

5 BOSTON WAY'S
CHICKEN OLD VIRGINIA

Chicken:

8 4-ounce boneless chicken
 breasts
8 thin ham slices
1 cup instant grits,
 prepared

2 tablespoons peanuts
6 saltine crackers
$\frac{1}{2}$ cup bread crumbs

Trim and pound chicken breasts until thin. Place a slice of ham on each breast and place 2 tablespoons of grits on the ham. Tucking in the ends of the breast, roll the breast to encase the grits and ham. Crumble peanuts in a food processor. Add saltines and bread and process until smooth. Roll chicken breasts in breading mixture, coating well. Bake in a preheated 425-degree oven for 14 to 16 minutes. Remove and slice.

Peanut Sauce:

2 tablespoons butter
$\frac{3}{4}$ cup minced onion
$\frac{1}{4}$ teaspoon garlic salt
1 teaspoon thyme
$1\frac{3}{4}$ teaspoons black pepper
$\frac{1}{4}$ cup white wine
$\frac{1}{2}$ cup crunchy peanut
 butter

$1\frac{1}{2}$ tablespoons lemon juice
1 cup melted butter
1 cup chicken stock
 (homemade or
 commercial)
$\frac{3}{4}$ teaspoon salt

Melt 2 tablespoons of butter in a saucepan and sauté onion until browned. Add garlic salt, thyme, pepper and wine.

151

Reduce until mixture reaches syruplike consistency and stir in peanut butter. Place mixture in food processor and purée. While processor is running, slowly add lemon juice, 1 cup of melted butter, chicken stock and salt. Blend until smooth. Ladle peanut sauce over chicken. Serves 8.

5 BOSTON WAY'S SALMON FILLET WITH WARM TARTAR SAUCE

Salmon:

2 eggs
¾ cup milk
1 cup plain flour
1 cup cornmeal

6 5-ounce boneless salmon fillets
3 to 4 tablespoons butter

Whisk eggs and milk in a bowl. Set aside. Mix flour and cornmeal in a separate bowl. Dip salmon into egg mixture and then into flour mixture. Melt butter in a sauté pan over medium-high temperature. Add salmon and sauté for about 6 to 8 minutes until salmon flakes easily.

Warm tartar sauce:

1 tablespoon caper juice
¼ cup capers
¼ cup minced onions
¾ teaspoon chopped dill pickles
¾ teaspoon green peppercorns

pinch of garlic
⅛ teaspoon salt
2 tablespoons lemon juice
⅛ cup white wine
¼ cup heavy cream
1¼ cups sour cream

Mix all ingredients in a saucepan and heat until warm. Ladle over salmon. Serves 6.

DEERPARK
Asheville

DEERPARK

In the 1880s, George Vanderbilt instructed landscape designer Frederick Law Olmstead to set aside an area of his Biltmore Estate as a deer preserve. Today, Vanderbilt's Deerpark is approached by a winding three-mile drive through a forest with pools, springs, and streams. The rolling landscape of the Smoky Mountains subtly hides the castlelike Biltmore House, lending the illusion of a fairy tale. Deerpark's building, which has such English touches as a half-timbered and pebble-dash facade, was originally Biltmore's dairy barn. Vanderbilt's interest in self-sufficiency and the proper use of land is responsible for the dairy products which continue to be produced by the Biltmore Dairy and which you can enjoy when you visit Deerpark.

You may also sip one of the excellent wines made on the Biltmore Estate. On my initial visit, the winery was newly in operation, but it is now nine years old and has expanded its market to seven states. If you've been through their wine-tasting rooms, you've probably discovered your own favorite, I'm partial to their Chardonnay.

I lunched alfresco in the restaurant's flower-filled garden courtyard. My favorite entrée is their Sliced Breast of Cold Duckling with Westphalian Ham, a tastefully inventive arrangement served with herbed cream cheese, orange sections, grapes, creamed horseradish sauce and melba toast. Another good choice is the Spinach and Smoked Turkey Salad Princess, which features their Herbed Bacon Dressing.

For dessert, the homemade Apple Honey Nut Ice Cream is a treat by itself, but when it's combined with vanilla and chocolate in an éclair shell under a blanket of hot fudge as their Frozen Chocolate Eclair, the taste is beyond compare. Fresh, seasonal Berry Crêpes are another favorite, as are the fresh Peach Pie and Key Lime Pie.

The Vanderbilt tradition has remained intact under current owner William Amherst Vanderbilt Cecil, grandson of George Vanderbilt. Do set aside enough time to tour the majestic Biltmore House, Gardens, and Winery and to dine at Deerpark.

Deerpark is located on the Biltmore Estate, which is off U.S. 25 at Asheville. Lunch is served (to Biltmore Estate visitors only) from 11:00 a.m. until 3:00 p.m. daily, from March 1 through December 31. Deerpark serves dinner only to large private parties. For reservations call (704) 255-1140.

DEERPARK'S KEY LIME PIE

2 cans sweetened condensed milk	9-inch deep-dish graham cracker piecrust
¾ to 1 cup lime juice	whipped cream
2 egg yolks	

Preheat oven to 400 degrees. Thoroughly mix sweetened condensed milk with ½ cup of the lime juice. Add more lime juice to taste. Add egg yolks, blending to incorporate. Pour mixture into pie shell. Turn oven off and place pie in oven immediately. Bake 5 to 6 minutes until set. Remove from oven and cool. Cover and refrigerate; pie freezes well for a day or so. Before serving, garnish with whipped cream if desired. Yields 1 pie.

DEERPARK'S HERBED BACON DRESSING

½ cup bacon grease	¾ teaspoon sage
½ cup crumbled bacon	¾ teaspoon salt
2 cups water	½ teaspoon pepper
½ cup wine vinegar	¾ teaspoon Dijon mustard
1 teaspoon chopped garlic	2 tablespoons water
6 tablespoons chervil	2 tablespoons cornstarch

Place bacon grease in a medium saucepan. Add bacon, 2 cups of water, vinegar, garlic, sugar, chervil, sage, salt, pepper and mustard and stir over medium heat. Bring to a boil. Combine 2 tablespoons of water with cornstarch and add to bacon mixture; cook only until dressing begins to thicken. Pour over lettuce or spinach. Yields 1 quart.

DEERPARK'S CAJUN BEEF,
BEER AND CHEESE SOUP

7½ cups water
2 ounces beef base
½ teaspoon black pepper
¼ teaspoon white pepper
⅓ teaspoon red pepper
1 celery stalk, chopped
1 small onion, chopped
6 ounces or more beef,
    diced

½ green pepper, seeded
    and chopped
½ cup all-purpose flour
½ cup butter
1 cup or more cheddar or
    Gouda cheese, shredded
¼ cup or more beer

Boil water with beef base and black, white and red peppers in a 5-quart Dutch oven or other large pot. Add celery, onion, beef and green pepper. Cook at a simmering boil until beef is tender. Reduce heat to medium-low. Replace any water that has boiled away. Combine flour and butter in a sauté pan and stir over low heat. Add flour mixture to soup, 1 tablespoon at a time, stirring after each addition. Add cheese and stir until melted and combined with other ingredients. Before serving, add beer and stir only until heated through. Yields about 2 quarts.

THE MARKET PLACE
Asheville

THE MARKET PLACE The most interesting historical tidbit about the building from the early twenties that now houses The Market Place restaurant is that it was once a printing shop whose owners fired Walt Disney. Speculations concerning his termination are limited only by your imagination, but the favored explanation is that printers use artists primarily for printing, not cartooning.

I am happy to report, however, that the owners and renovators of the Market Place were not handicapped by the shortsightedness of the previous owners. Their conversions have given the restaurant a sophisticated tropical décor that blends successfully with its classic continental cuisine. The most attractive feature of this unusual décor is the wainscoting made of terra-cotta tiles surrounded by and Art Nouveau metalwork that once decorated railroad dining cars. I really loved the comfortable bamboo chairs, which are smartly cushioned in muted tropical prints. Circle down the stairs and you are greeted by an entirely different but equally pleasant atmosphere in The Grill Room.

Upstairs amidst the bamboo, I was made to feel, as the restaurant's motto suggests, that the Market Place was responsible for my well-being as long as I was under its roof. When I explained to the chef and co-owner, Mark Rosenstein, that I had been overindulging lately, he suggested the Poached Trout and said I couldn't have anything lighter without eating air. He was right, and my palate was not underprivileged with this choice. For a different dining taste you might try the Grilled Lamb or Chicken St. James.

The underground wine cellar is kept at sixty-two degrees. In the amended words of the poet Henry Aldrich, The Market Place suggests, "If all be true I do think, there are three reasons we should drink: Good wine—a friend—or being dry." On that, and the too-delicious-to-describe multilayer Marjolaine Cake, I will bid you a sumptuous dining experience at The Market Place.

The Market Place is located at 10 North Main Street in Asheville. Dinner is served from 6:00 until 10:00 p.m. Monday through Saturday from April 15 to October 31, and from 6:00 until 9:30 p.m. Monday through Saturday from November 1 to April 14. For reservations call (704) 252-4162.

THE MARKET PLACE'S MARJOLAINE CAKE

Almond praline:

1 cup sugar **½ cup almonds, toasted**

Caramelize sugar. Pour into pan; cool and grind with almonds. Cover and set aside.

Vanilla cream:

2 cups whipping cream **1 teaspoon vanilla**
4 tablespoons sugar

Whip cream with sugar and vanilla until thick peaks form. Place in a strainer and let sit overnight at 65 degrees.

Meringues:

⅝ cup almonds, toasted **¼ cup plain flour**
⅞ cup filberts, toasted **9 egg whites**
¼ cup sugar

Grind together filberts and almonds; add sugar and flour. Whip egg whites until stiff and fold nut mixture carefully into them, blending thoroughly. Line two 12- by 18-inch baking sheets with silicone baking paper. Draw two rectangles 4 by 16 inches on each piece of paper. Divide mixture into four equal parts on the sheets and spread with a spatula to fill rectangles. Meringue should be ½ inch thick. Bake at 300 degrees for 1 hour and 15 minutes to 1 hour and 45 minutes, or until slightly crispy. Cool and preserve.

Chocolate cream:

1½ cups semi-sweet **1¼ cups sour cream**
  chocolate

On the next day, combine chocolate and sour cream in a double boiler and heat until chocolate melts; keep warm. Mix ½ cup almond praline into ½ cup chocolate mixture.

To assemble cake, place a layer of meringue on a serving

dish. Spread evenly with all of chocolate and praline mixture. Top with second meringue and spread with ⅓ of chocolate and sour cream mixture. Refrigerate 10 minutes, then place third meringue on top and spread all of vanilla cream. Refrigerate 10 to 15 minutes, then top with last meringue and cover cake completely with remaining chocolate and sour cream mixture. Refrigerate for 12 to 24 hours before serving. Serves 16 to 20.

THE MARKET PLACE'S
GRILLED LAMB WITH MUSTARD

1 leg of lamb, deboned,
   butterflied, and cut into
   ½-inch steaks
2 tablespoons olive oil
2 tablespoons chopped
   fresh oregano

salt and pepper
cognac
4 tablespoons Dijon
   mustard
Béarnaise sauce

With a brush, coat lamb steaks with olive oil. Place on grill. Sprinkle with half of the oregano, salt and pepper. Cook 6 to 8 minutes, until blood shows. Turn and sprinkle other side with oregano, salt and pepper. Cook 4 to 8 minutes, depending on degree of doneness desired. Sprinkle cognac over top and ignite. Spread mustard on top and serve with Béarnaise sauce. Serves 8.

WEAVERVILLE MILLING COMPANY
Weaverville

WEAVERVILLE
MILLING COMPANY

Remember Rosie the Riveter, the symbolic World War II woman who took the traditional male jobs that kept the factories producing while our boys were away? Weaverville Milling Company had its own version of Rosie in Margie Duff, who kept the mill wheel grinding out the community's flour and meal during the war years. It was an arduous task, but a combination of woman power and willpower kept the operation going.

Weaverville Milling Company is now a restaurant, but remnants of the operation that began in 1912 can still be found on the top floor of the mill. The equipment now enhances the restaurant's rustic décor and sets the stage for a participatory look backward. Guests at the restaurant are free to do more than just have a good meal.

Near our table on the main floor was an old jigsaw puzzle. Every now and then a diner would wander over and fit another piece into its place. On the mezzanine, which is decorated with handmade quilts that are for sale, an old-fashioned dollhouse waits for the amusement of children before or after dinner.

Lovely touches of the country are everywhere. Just as we were turning to our seats from our tour, a woman placed on our table one of the loveliest bouquets of wild flowers you could imagine. The colors of the flowers set off our yellow-and-white checked tablecloth, the yellow pine walls, and the original oak floor.

The menu contained so many of my favorites that I had a hard time making a decision—until I found the Chicken with Raspberry and Rhubarb Sauce. What could be more unusual! The dish was so delicious that I tried to include the recipe here, but neither the chef nor I could figure out a way to break it down to family-size proportions.

My daughter Heather chose the very hearty V.I.P. Sandwich, prime rib au jus on toast with country fried potatoes. If you are trying to take it on the light side, the Vegetarian Lasagne might be a good suggestion, or Fresh Mountain Trout broiled in a Lemon and Herb Sauce.

Dieters beware: No meal at Weaverville would be complete without the desserts that have made the restaurant famous. They originated from old local recipes, but each has been given a creative twist under owners Sally and Kevin Smith. The freshest fruit of the season made the Blueberry and Peach Cobbler a standout, especially when topped with Homemade Vanilla Ice Cream; but a taste of Heather's Oatmeal Pie—reminiscent of a pecan pie—made that recipe a must.

I declined the special wine of the day because the homemade apple juice seemed exactly appropriate to this homespun experience. Guests under sixteen or over seventy-five receive a complimentary Slushy, an icy drink of 7-Up and grenadine. This is a terrific treat for all ages and will add a refreshing note to any hot summer day.

Weaverville Milling Company reminds me of an unpolished gem that turns up in a rock collector's pan: a treasure sparkling within a rough exterior.

Weaverville Milling Company is located on Reems Creek Road in Weaverville, ten minutes north of Asheville. Dinner is served from 5:00 to 9:00 p.m., daily except Wednesdays from April to January, and Thursday through Sunday in February and March. The restaurant closes for a couple of weeks in June. For reservations call (704) 645-4700.

WEAVERVILLE MILLING COMPANY'S
PEACH AND BLUEBERRY COBBLER

2 cups fresh peaches, sliced	3 tablespoons margarine,
1 cup fresh blueberries	melted
1 teaspoon cinnamon	1 cup white sugar
1 tablespoon lemon juice	1/2 cup brown sugar
1 cup flour	1/2 cup milk
1 teaspoon baking powder	1 tablespoon cornstarch
1/2 teaspoon salt	1 cup boiling water

Grease a 9- by 9-inch pan and fill with fruit. Sprinkle cinnamon and lemon juice over fruit. Mix flour, baking powder and salt. Cream margarine, brown sugar and 1/2 cup white sugar. Sift dry ingredients into creamed mixture, alternately adding milk; mix well. Spread over fruit. Sift ½ cup white sugar with cornstarch and sprinkle over batter. Pour boiling water over pie. Bake at 350 degrees for about 1 hour. Serves 8 to 10.

WEAVERVILLE MILLING COMPANY'S OATMEAL PIE

1 9-inch pie shell, unbaked
¼ cup margarine, melted
½ cup brown sugar
1 cup white corn syrup
1 cup raw oatmeal

3 eggs
½ teaspoon ground cloves
½ teaspoon cinnamon
¼ teaspoon salt

With electric mixer cream butter and sugar together; add all other ingredients and mix well. Pour into unbaked pie shell and bake at 350 degrees for approximately 1 hour.

WEAVERVILLE MILLING COMPANY'S SLUSHY

6 ounces 7-Up
1 tablespoon grenadine

2 ounces club soda
6 ice cubes

Place all ingredients in blender and mix until frothy. Serves 1.

NU·WRAY INN
Burnsville

NU-WRAY INN

Protected in a pocket of the Blue Ridge Mountains is an 1833 inn whose original eight rooms were erected with logs and held together with locust pins. When you arrive at the Nu-Wray Inn, which has been in the Wray family for the past hundred years, it will take a moment to remember that you are still in the twentieth century. I am sure you will soon welcome the adjustment from the prepackaged pleasures of the city to this oasis of gentility.

Comfortable rockers invite you to sit on the sprawling veranda, or you may meander past the parlor's stone fireplace to the upstairs drawing room known as the Blue Room. Unlike many drab Colonial colors, the forget-me-not blue of the doors and mantel illumines the room's rich Victorian furniture and its assortment of musical instruments, not the least of which is a square rosewood piano and a Reginaphone music box.

Don't become so removed from time in the graciousness of this room that you miss the chime of the dinner bell, because the amount and variety of food set upon the lace-covered tables is reminiscent of a medieval banquet. My first visit was on Thanksgiving. Need I say more? Only a masochist could diet in the presence of those temptations. My family indulged, to speak euphemistically, in Country Ham, Fried Chicken, Turkey, Dressing, Corn Pudding, Green Beans, Candied Yams, Relish, and mouth-watering hot Biscuits dripping with butter and honey, topped off with homemade dessert.

Later, when I asked what was enjoyed most, I received a chorus of "Everything!" In the summer you can diet on the smothered lettuce salad, but my advice is this: Enjoy the banquet and then hike for two to three hours, if you can still move.

The Nu-Wray Inn is located on the Town Square in Burnsville. Breakfast is served at 8:30 a.m., and supper at 6:00 p.m. Monday through Saturday. Sunday dinner is served at 1:00 p.m. For reservations call (704) 682-2329.

NU-WRAY INN'S TIPSY CAKE

Cake:

3 eggs	1½ cups flour
1 cup sugar	2 heaping teaspoons baking
4 tablespoons cold water	powder

Sift flour and baking powder together twice. Beat eggs and sugar together until light; add water and flour alternately. Bake in two greased and floured cake pans at 350 degrees for 25 to 30 minutes.

Custard:

1 quart milk	5 tablespoons sugar
5 eggs, minus whites of 2	1 tablespoon cornstarch
eggs	1 teaspoon vanilla

Bring milk to a boil. Beat eggs. Mix eggs, sugar and cornstarch into boiling milk. Remove from heat and stir in vanilla. Let cool until thick.

Toppings:

½ pint whipping cream	⅔ cup sliced almonds,
2 egg whites	toasted
½ cup good wine, such as	any red jelly
sherry	

Whip cream with egg whites until stiff. To assemble cake, place one layer of cake in a large, deep bowl and moisten with wine. Cover top with almonds; add half of boiled custard. Repeat with second layer. Pile topping high on the last layer of the cake. Place bits of red jelly on top.

NU-WRAY INN'S SYLLABUB

1 quart cream, 24 hours old	½ cup grape juice, or ¼
1 cup fresh milk	cup orange juice
1 cup sugar	½ cup sherry
1 teaspoon vanilla	

Chill all ingredients. Place in a large bowl, and beat with eggbeater until frothy. Serve immediately. Serves 10.

NU-WRAY INN'S CREAM GRAVY

4 tablespoons bacon grease   1/2 cup milk
3 tablespoons flour   1/2 cup water
1/2 teaspoon salt

Heat bacon grease. Add flour and salt; stir until it begins to brown. Add milk and water, and boil until thick. Serve with steamed rice. Yields 1 cup.

NU-WRAY INN'S SOUR CREAM PIE

1 cup sour cream*   1/2 teaspoon nutmeg
3/4 cup sugar   1/2 teaspoon ground cloves
2 eggs   1 9-inch pie shell, unbaked
pinch of salt   whipped cream, sweetened
1 teaspoon cinnamon   1/2 cup chopped pecans

Mix sugar and sour cream together; add slightly beaten eggs, salt and spices. Pour into unbaked pie shell and bake at 425 degrees for 8 to 10 minutes. Reduce heat to 325 degrees and bake another 20 minutes or more. Sweetened whipped cream and pecans may be placed on top. Yields 1 pie.

*A cup of undiluted evaporated milk plus one tablespoon of vinegar may be used in place of sour cream.

NU-WRAY INN'S PEAR HONEY

7 pounds pears, nearly ripe   1 large can shredded
5 pounds sugar   pineapple

Peel and core pears. Put through largest hole of meat grinder or in food processor. Mix sugar with pears; boil 50 minutes, stirring toward the last to prevent sticking. Add pineapple and boil about 10 minutes longer, until syrup thickens. Seal in sterile jars.

Good on vanilla ice cream. Yields 8 to 9 pints.

THE MAST FARM INN
Valle Crucis

THE MAST FARM INN

In 1810, Joseph Mast traded his rifle and dog for a two-thousand-acre tract of land in the secluded, rolling hills of Valle Crucis. He built a log cabin. Then, in 1885, Joseph's grandson Finley Mast built the current farmhouse. The home originally had six rooms with a detached kitchen, but it was later expanded to include thirteen bedrooms (with only one bathroom). Finley also built a structure to house the loom used by his wife, Josephine, who was a master weaver. In fact, some of Josephine Mast's work is still displayed at the Smithsonian.

During the early 1900s, this enterprising couple opened its home as a summer inn. Old-timers remember carloads of folks coming down on Sundays to stand around the springhouse and drink Aunt Josie's buttermilk. Author Elizabeth Gray Vining recalls in her book *Quiet Pilgrimage*, "Every day there appeared on the long, white-clothed table at which we all sat fried chicken, ham, homemade sausage, hot biscuits and spoon bread, home-churned butter. . . . Once I counted twenty different dishes."

A group of friends and I descended upon the inn's current owners, Sibyl and Francis Pressly, on a cool fall evening. A fire in the parlor took the chill from our bones before we joined guests at a family-style dinner. Having been raised on my grandmother's corn bread, I know really good corn bread when I taste it, and theirs would have pleased even my grandmother. I'm also high on unusual vegetable dishes, and their Enchiladas Suisa deserved lofty praise. Other guests enjoyed the fresh Mountain Trout, but I took only a delicious sliver for sampling so I could save room for dessert, a wonderfully moist Pineapple Creme Cake that was as authentically Southern as the Presslys' renovation of the inn.

My bedroom, which contained a medley of Pressly family antiques and mountain wild flowers, offered a soothing invitation to snuggle under their hand-stitched quilts. But how wonderful it was to wake up to the smell of baking biscuits and fruit breads. And unlike coffee, which never tastes as good as it smells, the fresh breads with homemade jam *did* taste as good as they smelled. As I devoured the tasty breads and fruit, I thought, "I'd never trade my dog for a piece of land, but I'm not too sorry that Joseph Mast did."

The Mast Farm Inn is located in Valle Crucis on State Road 1112, 3 miles from N.C. 105. Breakfast is served to lodging guests only. Dinner is served at 6:00 p.m. and at 7:45 p.m. Tuesday through Saturday. Sunday lunch is served at 12:30 p.m. and 2:30 p.m. For reservations call (704) 963-5857.

THE MAST FARM INN'S
PINEAPPLE CREME CAKE

Cake:

1 cup margarine, softened	3 cups self-rising flour
2 cups sugar	1 cup milk
3 eggs	1 teaspoon vanilla

Cream margarine and sugar; add eggs one at a time. Add flour gradually, alternating with milk. Add vanilla and beat well. Turn into 3 greased and lightly floured 8-inch cake pans. Bake at 350 degrees for 35 minutes.

Filling:

1 20-ounce can crushed pineapple	1/3 cup sugar

Combine pineapple and sugar in saucepan and boil for 7½ minutes, stirring to prevent sticking. Set aside.

Frosting:

1/3 cup margarine, melted	2 cups confectioners sugar
1 8-ounce package cream cheese	

Cream margarine and cream cheese, adding sugar until well mixed. Pierce each layer of the cake with fork so filling can seep through. To stack cake, spread 1/3 of the filling on the bottom layer, add second layer, and add another 1/3 of the filling. Add final layer and remaining 1/3 of filling. Frost top and sides. Yields 1 cake.

THE MAST FARM INN'S
ENCHILADAS SUISA

½ cup butter
¾ cup plain flour
2 cups milk
2 4-ounce cans chiles
2 chopped jalapeños, fresh
　or commercial
1 teaspoon salt
½ teaspoon white pepper

1 teaspoon powdered garlic
2 tablespoons olive oil
1 medium onion, chopped
2 pounds spinach, cooked
1 pound Swiss cheese,
　grated
10 flour tortilla shells

In a saucepan, melt butter and add flour gradually, stirring into a roux. Heat milk in separate pan until warm. Add milk to roux over low heat, stirring until creamy. Thin with water if too thick. Add chiles, jalapeños, salt, pepper, and garlic to mixture, stirring until incorporated. Set aside. Heat olive oil and sauté onions until tender; add spinach and cook 5 minutes, stirring in 1 cup of sauce. Grate cheese and place down the center of tortilla shells. Add spinach and onion mixture and another layer of cheese to each shell. Roll up tortillas. Place Tortillas on 2 13- by 9- by 2-inch pans. Ladle extra sauce and sprinkle more cheese on each. Bake at 375 degrees for 15 to 20 minutes until golden brown. Serves 10.

GREEN PARK INN
Blowing Rock

GREEN PARK INN   Prepare to be pleasurably pampered when you enter the Victorian-style Green Park Inn, with its abundance of latticework and white wicker furniture. Even in the winter the lobby resembles a burst of spring, with its bright green and yellow flowered décor. The green is, of course, symbolic of the Green family, whose seven brothers built their inn a hundred years ago right on the eastern continental divide.

The lounge, called The Divide, is bisected by the line. It is one of the enhancing additions that came with the inn's renovation in 1977. I was heartened to see that the renovators were careful to retain the charming traditions that reigned during the South's era of graciousness, particularly in the multileveled dining room. There, dark green velvet chairs and white damask tablecloths are positioned at one end of the dance floor, where weekend dancing is enjoyed to the tunes of bygone days, as well as to those of the present time.

Since the menu changes often it is difficult to know which of Chef George Meyers's offerings of steak, chicken, pork, seafood, homemade soups, fresh vegetables, home-baked rolls, and salads will appeal to you. I thought the Stuffed Pork Chops and Onion Rolls were the best until, on another occasion, I found the Coq au Vin to be so magnificent that I persuaded them to share the recipe with us. Obviously I wasn't dieting, because I went right on to Coconut Cake, which was better than my grandmother's.

The best time to enjoy the Green Park is during the celebrated Sunday buffet. It is the most dazzling array of gastronomical and visual delights around. Fresh flowers in an ice-sculpture vase grace tables of tempting morsels arranged in silver chafing dishes. Don't try to resist even one of the four tables that are laden with preparations responsible for fantasy dreaming. Everything is delicious, but the seafood salad is such a winner that repeat diners check to make sure it is on the agenda before making reservations. An important dividend is that the buffet easily accommodates most diets, or you can order broiled beef or seafood.

With the quality of food and splendor that are synonymous with Green Park, it isn't surprising that in the past hundred years the inn has given refuge to presidents from Wilson to Ford. This is a comfortable place where world leaders have been found playing cards in the kitchen with the chef.

Green Park is located on U.S. 321 Bypass in Blowing Rock. Breakfast is served from 7:30 to 9:30 a.m., lunch from noon to 2:00 p.m., and dinner from 6:00 to 10:00 p.m. The Sunday buffet is served from 11:00 a.m. to 2:00 p.m. For reservations call (704) 295-3141.

GREEN PARK INN'S SEAFOOD SALAD

¼ pound langostinos
¼ pound Alaskan shrimp
¼ pound Alaskan king crab
 or (Atlantic snow crab)
½ cup diced peeled celery
½ cup diced onions
juice of 1 lime
⅔ cup mayonnaise

¼ teaspoon white pepper
½ teaspoon salt
dash of Worcestershire
 sauce
bib lettuce
black olives
sliced lemons

Boil seafood; cool and squeeze water from seafood. Mix seafood, celery, onions, lime juice and seasonings. Refrigerate. Serve on lettuce and garnish with olives and lemon slices. Yields 1 pound.

GREEN PARK INN'S STUFFED PORK CHOPS

4 to 6 lean pork chops
1 quart pork gravy (use 2
 packages of mix)
1 pound bread
3 eggs
1 cup chicken stock

1 sausage link
3 slices bacon, cooked
¼ cup diced celery
¼ cup diced onions
½ teaspoon sage
salt and pepper

Mix bread, eggs, chicken stock, sausage, bacon, celery, onions and seasonings to make dressing. Slice pork chops in center but do not cut through; fill with dressing. Place in baking pan and cover with pork gravy. Cover with foil. Bake at 400 degrees for 45 to 60 minutes. Serves 4 to 6.

GREEN PARK INN'S COQ AU VIN

2 chickens, cut up
1/2 cup butter
1 dozen white mushrooms
7 cups chicken stock
1/2 cup flour

1/4 cup good white wine
1/4 pound salt pork
1 cup tiny whole onions
1/4 cup good brandy
1 1/2 cups uncooked rice

Brown chicken in butter, and remove to baking dish. Sauté mushrooms, salt pork and onions until onions are transparent; add to chicken. Make gravy from butter, flour, and 4 cups chicken stock. Add wine and brandy, and bring to a boil. Strain gravy over chicken, mushrooms, onions and salt pork. Cover with aluminum foil. Bake at 400 degrees for 45 minutes or until done. Cook rice in 3 cups chicken stock. Serve chicken over rice. Serves 6 to 8.

THE BEST CELLAR RESTAURANT
Blowing Rock

THE BEST CELLAR RESTAURANT

Had it not been for a lucky flip of a coin, The Best Cellar Restaurant would never have come into existence. If the coin had landed on its other side, owner Ira Wilson would be making toys in a Christian commune in Pennsylvania instead of serving food that he says is "made from the heart." But Ira won the toss that brought his family south. For a number of years, The Best Cellar was located in downtown Blowing Rock in a basement near a Christian bookstore operated by Ira's wife, Lani. Those were the restaurant's fledgling days, when the whole community pitched in with favorite recipes and managerial ideas to help the young couple become successful. The restaurant grew, as did the Wilson family. They eventually converted their 1938 log-cabin home into what is now the area's most sought-after restaurant. It took me three visits just to get a reservation.

And if you miss their sign or forget that the restaurant, which is also known as the Old Barnwell House, is hidden about two hundred yards up a winding road from the U.S. 321 bypass, you'll miss it. Backtrack if necessary, because this is a find!

When I visited, a fire was crackling in one of the restaurant's three fireplaces. A quilt hangs above the mantle of the former living room, with its old, cracked-beam ceiling. An arched doorway flanked by stained-glass doves leads onto an enclosed patio. In summer the patio would be my choice, but the fireplace in the former back bedroom signaled an intimate appeal on that fall evening.

My yellow tablecloth was winsomely set with peach-colored Fiesta ware, a wooden candlestick and amber-colored wineglasses. Except for the wineglasses, I could have been eating in my grandmother's kitchen. The décor is old-fashioned but the food isn't. Thought, imagination and energy are apparent. Each dish looked as if it had been posed for a food magazine, including the salad, served with a special Poppyseed dressing or their creamy Vinaigrette Dijon. I did some heavy sampling of their Shrimp Provençal and Veal Scallopini a la Creme. The key to the robust taste of the shrimp is the brandy sauce. The reason for the veal's success is harder to pinpoint. The cream sauce is delicate, which allows the veal to stand on its own admirable merits. In some restaurants the vegetables are an afterthought, but not in The Best Cellar, as the Wilsons were once vegetarians. My next Thanksgiving dinner will include Lani's marvelous Stuffed Zucchini. The Parsley Potatoes, Rice and home-baked Bread are equally satisfying, but the restaurant's pièce de résistance is its Banana Cream Pie. This rich and creamy wonder embodies the restaurant's philosophy—superb ingredients imaginatively and lovingly woven into a soul- and appétite-nurturing experience.

The Best Cellar Restaurant is located off the U.S. 321 bypass in Blowing Rock. Call for directions. Dinner is served from 6:00 p.m. until 9:30 p.m. Monday through Saturday from May until November. Dinner is served on Friday and Saturday during the winter. For reservations call (704) 295-3466.

THE BEST CELLAR'S
STUFFED ZUCCHINI

5 medium zucchini,
  parboiled
1 cup medium-sharp
  cheddar cheese, grated
2 ounces cream cheese,
  softened
3 tablespoons butter
2 cups Spanish onions,
  chopped
$\frac{1}{4}$ to $\frac{1}{3}$ cup pecans,
  chopped

2 heaping tablespoons dill
2 heaping tablespoons
  sweet basil
$\frac{1}{2}$ cup zucchini pulp
$\frac{1}{3}$ cup whole-wheat bread
  crumbs
3 to 4 slices Swiss cheese
paprika to taste

Slice zucchini lengthwise. Scoop pulp from zucchini and strain through cheesecloth. Set aside $\frac{1}{2}$ cup of pulp. Mix cheddar cheese and cream cheese in a medium-sized bowl. Heat butter in a skillet and sauté onions until very brown. Mix in pecans, dill, sweet basil and $\frac{1}{2}$ cup zucchini pulp.

Bind with bread crumbs. Stuff zucchini shells with mixture and top with Swiss cheese. Bake in a preheated 400-degree oven for 15 to 20 minutes. Sprinkle paprika on top. Serves 5.

THE BEST CELLAR'S
SHRIMP PROVENCAL

4 tablespoons butter,
  chilled
½ cup dry sherry
1 cup Spanish onion,
  chopped
3 large cloves garlic,
  minced
1 pound large shrimp,
  deveined with tails left
  intact

3 medium tomatoes,
  skinned, seeded and
  chopped
½ cup fresh basil or ½
  teaspoon dried basil
salt to taste
white pepper to taste
4 tablespoons butter
1 cup scallions, chopped

Place 4 tablespoons of chilled butter in a cold skillet with sherry. Blend as heat is slowly raised to medium-high, being very careful not to let sauce break down. Add onion and garlic and sauté until almost tender. Add shrimp, tomatoes and basil and sauté until shrimp just begin to turn pink. Add salt and pepper. Add 4 tablespoons of butter and stir in scallions, sautéing until shrimp is done. Place mixture on warm plates, with rice on the side. Decorate with edible flowers. Serves 4.

THE RAGGED GARDEN INN AND
RESTAURANT
Blowing Rock

THE RAGGED GARDEN INN AND RESTAURANT

For year, tourists strolling the sidewalks of downtown Blowing Rock have stopped to admire the roses growing along the stone walls that surround this grand old home. Built in 1900 by the Washburn family of Charlotte, the structure known today as The Ragged Garden was one of Blowing Rock's first summer homes. From the minute you enter the stone driveway, you are immediately struck by the extensive stonework. There is a stone porte-cochère, where guests in earlier days were delivered from their horse-drawn carriages. There are stone porches on two sides and a stone terrace extending all along the front of the house.

The outside of the house is covered in chestnut bark, which was traditional in early resort homes in the area. Since a blight destroyed most of the local chestnut trees, the irreplaceable shingles lend a distinctive architectural ambience to the Ragged Garden. The stone walls surrounding the front and side of the Ragged Garden are the perfect complement to the beautiful gardens and trees that landscape the one-acre setting.

In 1983, Joyce and Joe Villani were looking for a place to open a restaurant in the mountains of North Carolina. The Blowing Rock home had been unoccupied for three years, but they could immediately see its potential. Joyce and Joe have transformed this town landmark into a warm, inviting restaurant and inn. The two public dining rooms have large, native-stone fireplaces, beautiful chestnut paneling, and chestnut-boxed ceiling beams. The main dining area also features a stone staircase leading to the five charming rooms that can be rented by overnight guests. There is a private dining room in what used to be the family's library, and on pleasant summer evenings the Villanis offer candlelight dining on the stone terrace.

The restaurant features classic continental cuisine, with a strong emphasis on northern Italian dishes, a reflection of Joe's family heritage. Although Joe changes the menu every night with his special offerings, there is also a set menu that suggests the influence Joe's family has had on his culinary talents. The set menu features Linguine al Pesto from his cousin Emma, Papa's Saltimbocca alla Romana, and Mama's Cannelloni alla Bolognese.

Although his family has been involved in the restaurant business since coming to this country from Parma, Joe has established impressive credentials on his own. He majored in American history in college before leaving graduate school to begin his restaurant training at Sardi's Restaurant in New York City. Seven years later he purchased The Gaslight in Greenwich, Connecticut, which he owned for sixteen years. Before moving to Blowing Rock, he owned La Belle Verrière in Winter Park and The Driftwood Restaurant in Vero Beach, both in Florida. But now he and Joyce have found their dream come true, working and living on the premises of The Ragged Garden.

The Ragged Garden Inn and Restaurant is located one block off Main Street on Sunset Drive in Blowing Rock. Meals are served from 5:30 until 9:00 p.m. Wednesday through Sunday. For reservations call (704) 295-9703.

THE RAGGED GARDEN'S
SALTIMBOCCA ALLA ROMANA

8 slices veal, sliced thin and pounded	2 tablespoons butter
	8 thin slices prosciutto ham
Salt and pepper to taste	8 thin slices mozzarella
½ cup all-purpose flour	cheese

Preheat broiler. Sprinkle salt and pepper on each slice of veal. Dredge veal in flour; pat and remove excess flour. Melt butter in sauté pan over high heat. When butter foams, place veal in pan. Do not crowd. Sauté one minute each side. Place veal in ovenproof serving dish. Top with prosciutto and cheese. Place serving dish 4 inches under broiler just until cheese melts. Serve immediately. Serves 4.

THE RAGGED GARDEN'S
RISOTTO ALLA PANA

3 tablespoons butter
1 medium onion, chopped
   fine
1 cup uncooked rice,
   washed

4 to 5 cups chicken stock,
   warmed
1/2 cup heavy cream
4 to 5 teaspoons grated
   Parmesan cheese

Melt butter in a heavy pot over low heat. Add onion and cook until soft and translucent. Add rice and mix until rice is well coated with butter mixture, then add one cup stock and cook until rice absorbs all liquid. Continue adding stock one cup at a time until rice is cooked. Allow at least 30 minutes of cooking time for the rice. Stir in cream and cheese and serve in soup bowls. Serves 4.

THE RAGGED GARDEN'S
SPUMA DE ZAMBAIONE

4 egg yolks
4 tablespoons sugar
1/2 cup Marsala wine

2 cups heavy cream
2 ounces bittersweet
   chocolate, grated

Cream egg yolks and sugar in a double boiler. Add wine and whisk briskly, or use electric mixer on low speed. Heat, stirring continuously, until mixture is thickened to a ribbon consistency. Be careful not to boil. Remove pan from heat and let cool to room temperature. Whip cream and set aside. When egg mixture has cooled, fold in whipped cream and grated chocolate, reserving some for garnish. Serve in long-stemmed glasses. Serves 4 to 6.

DAN'L BOONE INN
Boone

DAN'L BOONE INN

After eating at the Dan'l Boone Inn, it's amazing that I can even spell the word *diet*. I ate with complete disregard of its meaning. I'll bet if such food had been served back in the 1930s, when this rambling old edifice operated as a hospital, poor appetites would have completely disappeared.

"Oh, but the food is embarrassingly simple," protested one of the inn's co-owners, Jim Paal, when I asked for his recipes. "It's nothing more than your mother prepares at home. But our box lunch is a real buy. When it's warmer, people take these boxes to a picnic in the area. That way they can escape the long lines and also enjoy a satisfying meal outdoors." Just for the record, that simple box contains two pieces of chicken, green beans, stewed apples, two home-made country biscuits, two plain biscuits, and home-baked cake. I can assure you that my mother never packed me a box lunch like that!

I would have liked to dine on the porch, which has a tree growing through its center, but the comforting stone fireplace in the knotty-pine dining room has more appeal on a winter day. The room, with its sagging floors, is decorated with an assemblage of functioning antiques that range from apple presses to clocks.

The waitress served us family-style, which means that the entire menu was placed upon our red tablecloth in bowls or platters, including three different meats. That allows a choice of whatever and how much you want to eat. My vote goes to the Country-style Steak, Black Cherry Preserves on hot Biscuits, and Strawberry Shortcake for dessert. Though not recommended for dieters, the Dan'l Boone Inn does offer a vegetarian meal at a reduced price. This is the kind of place where total strangers are apt to become well acquainted before the close of an evening.

The Dan'l Boone Inn is located at the junction of U.S. 321 and U.S. 421 in Boone. The inn is open in summer from 11:00 a.m. to 9:00 p.m. Monday through Friday, and from 8:00 a.m. to 9:00 p.m. Saturday and Sunday. The schedule varies through the winter. Reservations are not necessary, but for information call (704) 264-8657.

DAN'L BOONE INN'S CRANBERRY RELISH

1 12-ounce package fresh
  cranberries
10 apples

3 large oranges
2 16-ounce cans jellied
  cranberries

Grate fresh cranberries coarse and grate apples fine. (Can use food processor for this.) Dice peeled orange, removing any seeds. Mix all ingredients. Cover and refrigerate for 24 hours. This will keep from Thanksgiving through Christmas. Yields 1½ quarts.

DAN'L BOONE INN'S PRUNE CAKE

2 cups sugar
1 cup vegetable oil
3 eggs
2 cups self-rising flour
⅓ cup dry buttermilk
1 teaspoon nutmeg

1 teaspoon allspice
1 teaspoon cinnamon
1 junior-size jar of baby
  food prunes
1 cup chopped nuts

Mix sugar and oil; beat in eggs. Add flour, buttermilk, nutmeg, allspice and cinnamon. Blend together well. Stir in prunes and nuts. Bake in greased bundt pan or tube pan at 325 degrees for 1 hour and 15 minutes. Frost with buttermilk icing.

DAN'L BOONE INN'S BUTTERMILK ICING

⅓ cup buttermilk
¼ cup margarine

1 cup brown sugar
1 box confectioners sugar

Mix the buttermilk, margarine and brown sugar; bring to a boil. Slowly mix in the confectioners sugar. Blend thoroughly. Cool cake and frosting before spreading frosting.

DAN'L BOONE INN'S STEWED APPLES

5 McIntosh apples   **½ cup sugar**
6 tablespoons butter

Wash apples thoroughly. Core and section, and wash again. Melt butter in large, heavy pot. Place apples and sugar in pot; stew on high for a couple of minutes, then cook at medium high until soft but not mushy, about 8 minutes. (Add no water or other spices.) Serves 3 to 4.

GLENDALE SPRINGS INN
Glendale Springs

GLENDALE SPRINGS INN

Why would a Broadway producer want to open a gourmet restaurant in an 1895 inn in Glendale Springs? The atmosphere in Glendale Springs is not the same as New York's; the people are not the same; the landscape is not the same. The fact of the matter is that those differences provided the motivating factor for Gayle Winston to bid on General Adams' inn when it was auctioned.

When she learned that the house was to be auctioned off in pieces, Ms. Winston couldn't stand it. She had had no intention of buying it, but she couldn't bear to see something so fine dismembered. Not even knowing if she could finance the project, she asked the owners if they would accept a bad check until she could make more solid arrangements. They did, and she did, and the result is reminiscent of an exquisite piece of antique jewelry that has been polished and replaced in its familiar setting, and now proudly radiates its original elegance.

A large measure of this elegance cannot be attributed so much to the physical beauty of the inn; it comes, rather, from the remembrance that nineteenth-century society was based on the values of good taste. This taste is evidenced in so many ways at the inn, from the white linen tablecloths dressed with fresh flowers, to the iced tea served in wineglasses to the properly schooled service. These elements coalesce to produce an aura so distinctive that you will expect no less than epicurean food from chef Ted Herman. And in my opinion, you will not be disappointed.

At lunch, the Zucchini Soup with fresh herbs in a cream sauce was analogous to a full-bodied wine. It was followed by a light salad of greens and hearts of palm with a tiny violet perched in the center. The reason the Asparagus Omelet was so special was the fresh asparagus and fresh country eggs. Ever notice the difference a fresh egg makes? My dessert of Grapefruit and Kir Sorbets was the most refreshing experience of the entire meal. To be on the fair side, I did conduct a taste-test of the Coffee Almond Torte and the Triple Chocolate Napoleon, which are top candidates for any chocoholic.

The most popular appetizer for dinner is a Deep-fried

Herbed Crepe filled with Gruyere cheese, and this may be followed by a unique Tomato Vichyssoise. The most unusual entrée is the veal with bacon, herbs, and red wine in puff pastry. If you are in the mood for a lighter meal, the rainbow trout would be an excellent choice.

The inn has a "special occasion" license, meaning that wine and other alcoholic beverages can be arranged prior to your meal. Any time that you dine or overnight at the inn will be a special occasion because history and good taste have made it so. The inn is one block from the fresco of the Last Supper at Holy Trinity Episcopal Church.

Glendale Springs Inn is located on N.C. 16 at Glendale Springs. From April through October, lunch is served from noon until 2:00 p.m. Monday through Saturday, with a Sunday buffet from noon until 2:30 p.m.; dinner is served from 6:00 until 8:00 p.m. Sunday through Thursday and from 6:00 until 9:00 p.m. on Friday and Saturday. From November through January, meals are served on weekends only. Check for winter hours. For reservations call (919) 982-2102.

GLENDALE SPRINGS INN'S
ASPARAGUS OMELET

8 to 10 asparagus spears
melted lemon butter
salt
3 eggs
dash of fresh-ground
  pepper

dash of fresh-ground
  nutmeg
milk
fresh Hollandaise sauce
parsley

Steam asparagus; cut into one-inch pieces and drizzle with melted lemon butter and a sprinkle of salt. Set aside and keep warm. Lightly mix eggs, nutmeg, salt, pepper and milk. Melt butter in an omelet skillet and pour in egg mixture. With the back of a fork, lightly scramble the eggs. As soon as mixture begins to set, add asparagus to center and fold egg over asparagus. Divide into two equal portions and place on warm plates. Dress with a ribbon of freshly prepared Hollandaise sauce and garnish with parsley. Serves 2.

GLENDALE SPRINGS INN'S
GRAPEFRUIT SORBET

4 or more grapefruits   2 cups sugar
1 cup water

Squeeze 3 cups grapefruit juice and set aside. Place water and sugar in a small saucepan and bring to a rolling boil; cook until it forms a simple syrup. Add syrup to grapefruit juice and mix. Cover tightly and put in freezer. When firmly chilled, place in ice cream freezer and follow machine's instructions. You may freeze mixture in freezer for different consistency. Yields 10 to 12 scoops.

GLENDALE SPRINGS INN'S HERB BUTTER

½ cup butter   1 teaspoon chopped chives
2 tablespoons chopped   2 shallots, chopped
  fresh tarragon   6 parsley sprigs

Combine ingredients in food processor with steel blade or use electric mixer.

GLENDALE SPRINGS INN'S ZUCCHINI SOUP

1 large onion, chopped   2 cups vegetable broth or
2 cloves garlic, minced   beef stock
2 tablespoons herb butter   2 cups half-and-half
  (see recipe above)   2 tablespoons curry powder
4 cups zucchini, peeled and
  sliced thin

Sauté onions and garlic in herb butter. Cover and let sweat for 1 minute. Add zucchini and vegetable broth or beef stock. Cover and cook until tender. Drain and purée in blender. Return to saucepan and add half-and-half and curry. Heat through. Serves 8.

GREENFIELD RESTAURANT
West Jefferson

GREENFIELD RESTAURANT

As I sat sipping my coffee and gazing through a bay window at rolling green fields, I could easily understand how this rustic restaurant got its name. A moment later I was eating an overabundant breakfast of country ham, sausage, eggs, grits, gravy, strawberry preserves, and a batch of biscuits so good that they literally sent me into the kitchen for the recipe. Now I know why mountain people are so robust and healthy. Their plentiful natural resources sponsor these attributes.

Those natural resources were first recognized by the Cherokee Indians, who use a nearby spring and sheltered themselves inside a cave on Mount Jefferson. The cave, still rich in Indian artifacts, was discovered several years ago. Oldtimers of the region remember the covered wagons that sought refuge near the natural spring, where milk and butter were kept cool in a deep trough. It was nearby that Rufus McNeil built the white farmhouse that is now Greenfield. The date of the house, 1890, remains chiseled inside the fireplace.

During the McNeils' tenure, the land was used to farm, and chestnuts and chinquapins were gathered from the woods. Today, however, farming has been replaced by a full-scale recreation area. In addition to being served three meals a day at Greenfield, you can go camping, canoe, ride horseback, hike and swim. On alternate Saturday nights in the summer, you are welcome to attend an evening of square dancing or bluegrass music.

I am also pleased to report that Greenfield is another of the country-style restaurants where you can have a light fresh fruit salad or the Greenfield vegetable salad for lunch. Owners William and Jo Ann Woodie are happy to comply with your dietary requirements at dinner if you give them notice before you go. However, most people go to Greenfield for the fried chicken, country ham, and the other, simple, old-fashioned foods for which the restaurant is so famous. Once during dinner, the parking lot was packed not only with cars and motorcycles, but with two fire trucks, a helicopter, two horses, and a boat. A local reporter remarked, "People will come here by just about any mode of transportation that runs." After only one meal I can say "amen" to that remark.

Greenfield Restaurant is located one mile south of West Jefferson, off U.S. 221 and N.C. 163. It is open daily for breakfast from 7:00 to 10:00 a.m., for lunch from 11:00 a.m. to 4:00 p.m., and for dinner from 4:00 to 9:00 p.m. For reservations call (919) 246-9671.

GREENFIELD'S GLAZED CARROTS

1 pound carrots   ¼ cup sugar
¼ cup butter or margarine

Scrape carrots and cut diagonally. Heat salted water in a saucepan until boiling. Place carrots in water, reduce heat to medium, and cook until tender. Drain carrots. In same saucepan, melt butter and add sugar, stirring to combine. Add carrots and cook on low for 10 to 15 minutes. Serves 6 or more.

GREENFIELD'S BISCUITS

2 cups Southern Biscuit   1 tablespoon sugar
    self-rising flour   1 teaspoon baking powder
⅔ cup buttermilk   ⅓ cup margarine
⅔ cup sweet milk   ⅓ cup shortening

Mix flour, milk, sugar and baking powder. Work margarine and shortening into flour mixture. Cover well and refrigerate. Will keep for a day. Roll out on floured board and cut out with biscuit cutter. Bake at 450 degrees for 8 to 10 minutes. Yields 12 biscuits.

GREENFIELD'S RICE AND PINEAPPLE

3 cups uncooked white rice
½ cup margarine, melted
1 cup sugar

1 No. 2 can (2½ cups)
crushed pineapple
1 teaspoon salt

Cook rice; mix in margarine. Add sugar, pineapple and salt, and mix well. Serve hot. Serves 8 to 10.

SHATLEY SPRINGS INN
Crumpler

SHATLEY SPRINGS INN

Perhaps the food at Shatley Springs Inn is the principal drawing card today, but that was not always the case. The inn began in the early part of the century as a health resort.

The story concerning the origin of Shatley Springs Inn is recounted in a printed statement by Martin Shatley. He claims that for over seven years he had been so ill with consumption and other painful diseases that doctors pronounced him incurable. Believing that he was near death, Shatley bought a farm to provide for his family's welfare. Soon after the purchase of the farm, Shatley passed a spring on his land and stopped to bathe his inflamed face. He declared that in less than an hour the healing process had begun. After only a few days of bathing in the spring water, his fever disappeared, and in three weeks, he was well enough to do heavy farm labor. His statement further asserts that in the ensuing thirty-five years he witnessed the cure of people with skin diseases, rheumatism, and nervous disorders.

I was curious to see the spring providing these curative waters, which according to analysts is especially high in calcium, magnesium, and five other healthful minerals. But the aroma of fried chicken drew me into the dining room.

The man sitting next to my table said, "I bet you could have a good meal by eating the crumbs off this table." That expression intrigued me, but it wasn't long before my own table was crammed to the limit with dishes of food served "family-style." Shatley Springs offers what I would describe as country food that has been properly seasoned. Diners can choose among several entrées, and my favorite is the Chicken Pie. The cooks at Shatley vow that there isn't a cookbook or written recipe in the place, thus making it impractical for them to break down the recipes for me to test for an average-sized family. The fried chicken recipe is so secret that a waitress told me her mother had worked at Shatley for years and still didn't know it. The country hams are cured by the restaurant's owner, Lee McMillan, who sells them whole and by the pound, as well as by the plateful.

I did discover the secret that makes the vegetables tastier than mine. Those at Shatley are fresh or frozen and are cooked with half-and-half, real butter, and a little flour. What a difference the real thing can make. This just doesn't seem the type of place you'd think of for a dieter, but I was surprised that a cottage cheese and fresh fruit salad is available for lunch.

Saturday nights frequently feature country, bluegrass, or gospel music; but alcoholic beverages are never allowed. That philosophy seems in harmony with the healing minerals of the spring outside. Even today people come from distant states to haul away the mystical waters. There is no charge for the water, but a nominal fee is collected for an unused plastic jug to take it home in.

After my plentiful meal I was feeling no pain at all, but you never know what's in store, do you? So, yes, I brought home a gallon of Shatley Springs's water for, well, just in case.

Shatley Springs Inn is located on N.C. 16 at Crumpler. Breakfast is served from 7:00 to 9:00 a.m., and lunch begins at 11:00 a.m. Meals are served until 9:00 p.m., seven days a week, May through October. For reservations call (919) 982-2236.

SHATLEY SPRINGS INN'S RHUBARB COBBLER

2 cups chopped rhubarb
pinch of salt
1 cup sugar
1/2 teaspoon cinnamon
1/4 teaspoon nutmeg
1 teaspoon lemon juice

2 tablespoons butter
brown sugar
1 handful fresh
   strawberries, cut up
1 piecrust, unbaked

In covered saucepan, boil rhubarb in salted water until tender. Drain and place in greased shallow baking dish. Mix together sugar, cinnamon, nutmeg and lemon juice; mix with rhubarb. Dot with butter and sprinkle with strawberries. Cover with rolled-out piecrust and sprinkle brown sugar on top. Bake at 350 degrees about 40 minutes or until done. Serves 8 to 10.

SHATLEY SPRINGS INN'S COLESLAW

1 head cabbage
1/4 cup diced onion
1/2 cup milk
1/4 cup sugar

1/2 cup mayonnaise
2 tablespoons vinegar
1/2 teaspoon salt
1/2 teaspoon pepper

Shred cabbage. Add other ingredients and correct seasoning to taste. Cover and refrigerate. Serves 4.

SHATLEY SPRINGS INN'S CREAMED POTATOES

8 potatoes, peeled and
  quartered
1 teaspoon salt

1/4 cup butter
1 tablespoon or more flour
2 cups half-and half

In medium pot, place potatoes, salt and water to cover. Boil until potatoes are tender; drain. Add butter, half-and-half and flour, and mix until smooth and thick. Serve hot. Serves 6 to 8.

INDEX

Grilled Lamb with Mustard, Market Place 160
Kailua Steak, Country Squire 39
Lamb Zinfandel, Claire's 55
Pepper Steak, River Forest Manor 8
Pork with Mustard Sauce, La Résidence 68
Ribeye of Veal with Chanterelles, Lamplighter 103
Roast Pork Loin, Fearrington House 63
Runza, Academy 99
Saltimbocca Alla Romana, Ragged Garden 183
Stuffed Pork Chops, Green Park Inn 175
Veal Madeira Morel, Harvey House 31

Miscellaneous:
Asparagus Omelet, Glendale Springs Inn 191
Cornmeal Mush, Old Salem Tavern 80
Enchiladas Suisa, Mast Farm Inn 172
Original Dirigible, Clawson's 19

Seafood:
Broiled Barbecued Shrimp, Country Inn 119
Crab Cakes, Country Inn 120
Crab Imperial, Harvey House 32
Flounder Marguery, Stemmerman's 28

Marinated Shrimp Port Gibson, Tanglewood Manor House 95
Orange Roughy, Pine Crest Inn 123
Pamlico Crabmeat Casserole, River Forest Manor 8
Poached Fish Marseillaise, La Chaudière 87
Red Snapper Boursin, Tanglewood Manor House 95
Salmon Fillet with Warm Tartar Sauce, 5 Boston Way 152
Seafood Imperial, Grove Park Inn 148
Seafood Salad, Green Park Inn 175
Seafood with Spinach Fettucini, Sanderling Inn 4
Seviche, Stars 92
Shrimp in Caper Butter, Pelican 15
Shrimp Provençal, Best Cellar 180
Shrimp and Chicken Ariosto, Island Inn 12

SALADS, RELISHES, AND PICKLES:
Caesar Salad, Stars 92
Coleslaw, Shatley Springs Inn 200
Cranberry Relish, Dan'l Boone Inn 187
Cucumber Pickles, Pollirosa 75
Pickled Beets, Jarrett House 139